Teaching with Integrity
The ethics of higher education practice

Bruce Macfarlane

Teaching With Integrity seeks to bridge the gap currently separating the debate about teaching and learning in higher education from the broader social and ethical environment in which it takes place.

It provides practical advice on the real-life, messy moral dilemmas that confront university teachers on a daily basis. Such instances might include difficult relationships with colleagues or students, a decision over whether or not to extend a deadline, investigating suspected plagiarism or dealing with a complaint. Written in a scholarly yet accessible style, the book features illuminating case examples to encourage a practical, reflective approach.

The book also explores the wider debate surrounding moral integrity and how it should be maintained in the HE sector, analysing the pros and cons of a prescriptive professional code of conduct and ultimately putting the case for active development of professional virtues over bureaucratic recommendations.

Whether you are an HE lecturer requiring guidance on tackling an ethical dilemma or an HE manager looking for an insight into how best to maintain moral integrity within HE practice, this book will be required reading.

Dr Bruce Macfarlane is Reader in Higher Education at City University, London. He previously worked as a business and management lecturer and has published widely in the field of applied and professional ethics with particular reference to business and management education.

RoutledgeFalmer
Taylor & Francis Group

LONDON AND NEW YORK

For my mother and father

First published 2004 by RoutledgeFalmer
11 New Fetter Lane, London EC4P 4EE

Simultaneously published in the USA and Canada
by RoutledgeFalmer
29 West 35th Street, New York, NY 10001

RoutledgeFalmer is an imprint of the Taylor & Francis Group

Typeset by Saxon Graphics Ltd, Derby
Printed and bound in Great Britain by
TJ International Ltd, Padstow, Cornwall

British Library Cataloguing in Publication Data
A catalogue record for this book is available from the British Library

Library of Congress Cataloguing in Publication Data
Macfarlane, Bruce, 1961–
   Teaching with integrity : the ethics of higher education practice /
Bruce Macfarlane.
        p. cm.
Includes bibliographical references and index.
   ISBN 0-415-33508-6 (hard) -- ISBN 0-415-33509-4 (pbk.)
  1.   College teachers--Professional ethics--England--Case studies. 2.
College teaching--Moral and ethical aspects.   I. Title.
   LB1779.M32 2003
   174′ .937--dc21
                                                              2003013193

ISBN 0-415-33508-6 (hbk)
ISBN 0-415-33509-4 (pbk)

Contents

Foreword

In my judgement, in giving us this book, Bruce Macfarlane has performed a much-needed service. The central claim of this book, as I understand it, is that those who teach in higher education should reason *explicitly* about the value choices that they face in their working lives. It is accepted that intuitive choices are made all the time; what is less evident is those choices being made consciously and deliberately. If we wish to hold to the view that teaching in higher education is 'professional' in character, then we need – both individually and collectively – to be able to make the value basis of our actions explicit.

This is a bold set of claims, and for three reasons. Firstly, there are very few texts currently available that tackle this matter head-on. That, indeed, is a symptom of the difficulty that the book identifies. There has been a general reluctance among the academic community to address publicly and carefully the matter of the ethical basis of its actions. In going down this path, therefore, Macfarlane is breaking new ground, always a risky venture; but it is, surely, a highly worthwhile, if not downright necessary, venture.

Secondly, and following on, that there is a void in the literature on this matter is suggestive in its own right. There appears to be a reluctance to raise value issues, but why might that be? I am not sure that there is a clear answer to this question. It would be easy enough to reflect that the reluctance to pose value questions is characteristic of professional life in general. Value questions, of their nature, do not permit of straightforward answers. Even more, they are likely to generate dispute which may not yield to any definite resolution. 'Let sleeping dogs lie' is the motive at work here. While I believe that to be true, that this reluctance explicitly to identify and to address value issues is characteristic of professional life, I do not believe it to be the whole story.

My view is that there are features of academic life that compound this general reluctance. First, there is perhaps an intuitive sense that precisely because value issues do not permit of any straightforward resolution – as the examples in this book testify – to bring them to the surface could compromise the academic authority that those in higher education may feel is theirs. Secondly, there is at large in academic life still a tacit culture of 'value neutrality'. Frequently, of course, this idea is left behind, both in the classroom and in the committee meeting, as allegiances are admitted and even passions reveal themselves. But the idea of value neutrality persists, I think, as a kind of cultural residue. Lastly, the contemporary climate of 'performativity', with its insistence on demonstrable outcomes – preferably with a monetary gain – is threatening to reshape academic life in terms of an ideology of calculation. Bruce Macfarlane's book, therefore, implicitly challenges many of the deep-seated sentiments and beliefs about academic life.

But there is, to take these reflections just one step further, yet a third reason as to why this volume represents a bold set of claims. As I have just implied, the space into which Bruce Macfarlane is seeking to inject his ideas is not itself value neutral, much as it would claim to be. It is chock-full of values – both the newer ones, of growth, competition, economic strength, market performance – and those of earlier academic traditions, of truthfulness, of dialogue, understanding and mutual learning. And so, Bruce Macfarlane's plea in this book that those who work in academic settings should reflect *together*, and should see whether collectively a sense of academic virtue might be worked out, is tantamount to urging academic institutions to come clean about the value conflicts that persist within them under the surface of institutional life.

But it is more even than this: it is to invite the university effectively to have a dialogue with itself as to what kind of university it wishes to be: after all, in the single situation of determining the priority to be given to a single student and her or his pressing needs and in deciding how those needs are to be met (if at all) is raised pretty well all the value choices facing a university today. What values are to reside within it? How do they relate to each other? Can they be brought into any kind of coherent relationship with each other? If they cannot, how are such incommensurable values to be held together in the one institution, short of institutional fragmentation? Bill Readings talked of 'a university of dissensus': it may be that here, in this volume, Bruce Macfarlane gives us a hint of what such a university may look like, a university that is seriously intent on working through its value bases and value conflicts, conscious that there can never be any determinate resolution of those conflicts.

Teaching with Integrity, therefore, offers the implicit hope that individuals by themselves and in their immediate groups may be able to do justice to the idea of integrity in academic life. But it goes beyond this, for it also implies that it may be possible to do justice to the idea of integrity in relation to the university as such. In a world of dispute and contestability, it may be possible after all to do some justice to the idea that our universities can be institutions of integrity.

Ronald Barnett
Institute of Education, University of London

About the author

Bruce Macfarlane is Reader in Higher Education at City University, London. He was previously a lecturer in business and management for 13 years. He co-edited *Effective Learning and Teaching in Business and Management* (with Roger Ottewill) and is also the author of a wide range of articles on higher education and applied and professional ethics. He is co-editor of the *Journal of Business Ethics Education* and a member of the editorial board of a number of other academic journals, including *Teaching in Higher Education*.

Acknowledgements

I have many people to thank for helping me over the past three years with the research that formed the basis of this book. These included more than 200 academic staff undertaking a variety of educational development courses at both City University, London and Canterbury Christ Church University College, specially convened focus groups and workshop participants at recent conferences of the Institute for Learning and Teaching in Higher Education.

Moreover, I owe a particular debt to the following colleagues who took the time to write individual responses to the case study scenarios which appear in the book: Eddie Blass, Mike Cook, Sheila Counihan, Vaneeta D'Andrea, Nigel Duncan, Heather Fry, Geoff Haworth, Annie Huntington, Richard Keeble, Laurie Lomas, Susanna Martin, Gill Nichols, Jon Nixon, Roger Ottewill, Andrew Perkins, Sue Piotrowski, Jac Potter, Heather Purdey, Phil Race, Martin Rich, Stephen Rowland, Marion Stuart-Hoyle, Gwen van der Velden and Ann Wall. I also acknowledge, with thanks, permission to republish the case study in Chapter 5 that previously appeared in *Teaching in Higher Education*.

During the early part of the project, Jonathan Simpson, formerly of Kogan Page, was instrumental in encouraging me to begin work on the book and in co-ordinating individual responses to the case studies and, more latterly, Stephen Jones has helped me to see the project to completion. I would like to record my thanks to Jon Nixon and Ron Barnett, who also wrote the foreword. Their feedback enabled me to make a number of improvements to the original manuscript.

Finally, I would like to thank my wife, Alice, for her love, support and helpful suggestions in reading the manuscript.

Introduction

A complex reality

This is a book about the ethics of teaching in a higher education context. It is concerned with the real-life, everyday moral dilemmas that confront university teachers managing relationships with students and their colleagues. Such dilemmas may arise in various different contexts. These include classrooms and lecture halls, science laboratories, tutorial and meeting rooms, workplace environments and electronically, through the increasing use of e-mail and discussion boards.

In a formal sense, being a university lecturer is about teaching, tutoring, assessing and counselling students. It is also, for many, about administration and doing research. However, beyond the technical requirements of the job description it is about coping with a far more complex reality: facilitating discussion in a classroom environment, trying to decide when it is fair to extend an assignment deadline, responding to student evaluation of teaching, investigating when a student is suspected of cheating, running difficult meetings, dealing with complaints about colleagues and so on. Indeed, as the book will argue, the changing nature of modern higher education is having a significant impact on the ethical challenges which teaching academics confront.

Virtues for professional life

The focus of the book is on this difficult and 'messy' reality of professional life. It is concerned with the power and professional responsibilities of the university teacher rather than broader issues regarding the social rights agenda, such as widening participation or promoting equal opportunities, to which most modern governments and universities espouse commitment. This does not mean to imply that this social agenda is not important. It is simply that much attention has already been focused on these matters by other writers and researchers.

Instead, this book will present a series of moral dilemmas to the reader in the form of short 'case studies' based on the daily experiences of a number of fictitious university teachers. However, no attempt will be made to prescribe exact solutions to the challenges encountered. This is because ethics involves engagement with complex situations and making hard choices. This reality does not sit comfortably with formulaic solutions. While quandaries are used to reflect situations which arise in professional practice, these are not intended as a vehicle for generating over-simplified resolutions. Rather the book seeks to engage the reader in an ethical discussion while also reporting and analysing the reaction of those who have responded to these case studies in various contexts.

Many universities have now developed more detailed codes and guidelines for teaching staff in response to ethical and legal issues around the management of learning, especially student misconduct. While examples of these prescriptive approaches to decision making will be discussed, the shortcomings of this response to moral dilemmas will also be examined. The active development of professional 'virtues' will be recommended as an alternative to these more bureaucratic reactions to the changing nature of higher education. As Pincoffs (1986) has argued, moral reasoning needs to be intimately linked to moral character.

All the case studies used in the book have been evaluated by university lecturers via a combination of formal focus groups, workshops at academic conferences, educational development courses and through individual written response. This has been done to help ensure that the issues raised in the case studies are relevant to the real professional lives of teaching staff. It has also provided an insight into the ways in which teachers in higher education approach the resolution of ethical issues in their working lives. While most of the participants in these various discussions have been drawn from UK universities and colleges, this has included contributions from individuals with diverse backgrounds representing many different disciplinary, institutional, national and cultural traditions.

A special context

Why, though, it might be asked, do we need a book about the ethics of teaching in higher education? Well, while there is a small literature on the ethics of teaching, much of this is focused on compulsory age schooling (eg Gardner, Cairns and Lawton, 2000; Strike and Soltis, 1992). Moreover, most books on the ethics of teaching in universities and colleges are approached from a North American perspective (eg Fisch, 1996; Kennedy, 1997; Strike and Soltis, 1992; Whicker and Kronenfeld, 1994). Few focus on ethical issues in higher education from a European viewpoint. I am, however, indebted to the authors of these other studies for identifying some of the key moral dilemmas that appear in a fictionalized form within the case studies in this book.

Higher education also demands attention as a 'special' educational context. University life is traditionally associated with great privileges – of expression, curriculum design, research and teaching methods – but demands a high level of professional integrity if these freedoms are not to be too easily taken for granted. As Donald Kennedy has rightly pointed out, the flip side of academic freedom is academic duty (Kennedy, 1997). It is, perhaps, revealing that while the rights of academic staff are often debated there has been comparatively little attention paid over the years to their responsibilities. As an illustration of this bias, there are many books and articles about the concept of academic freedom but comparatively few that focus on ensuring that this principle applies equally to students.

It is also important that the role of ethics is given sufficient attention in the context of the recent growth of interest in teaching and learning issues in higher education. Here, there appears to be a growing 'peda-gogic gap' (Malcolm and Zukas, 2001) opening up between the burgeoning, technique-led literature on teaching and learning in higher education and books and articles focusing on the broader social, political, economic and ethical context of higher education. This phenomenon is in danger of divorcing ethics from the educational and professional development of the university teacher.

Finally, there is another contemporary reason why a book focusing on the ethics of teaching practice is needed. This is connected with the changing nature of teaching in higher education, partly in response to the need to cope with mass student numbers. While so-called massifi-cation (Scott, 1995) is long established in some higher education systems, such as the United States, it is a comparatively more recent development elsewhere, such as the UK and Australia. Partly as a result, students are now assessed in more varied ways: in the workplace, as members of a team, by each other and increasingly by coursework rather than formal examination. Teaching now takes place 'online' as well as in the lecture theatre or the seminar room and the Internet has opened up new possibilities for cheating, as well as learning. The parties to the educational exchange look very different from the way they did 20 or even 10 years ago. Students are more likely to be mature adults rather than teenagers fresh from school. Those doing the teaching are often employed part-time or on a short-term basis rather than enjoying the benefits of tenure or a permanent contract. They must cope with deteriorating staff–student ratios and pressures to continue to improve research performance in multi-mission institutions. This changing environment presents new challenges for teachers and students alike but, as I will argue, threatens to erode commitment to key virtues in relation to teaching.

Bridging the gap

In summary, this book seeks to bridge the pedagogic gap which currently divides much discussion and debate about teaching and learning in higher education from the broader social and ethical environment which lies outside the control of the individual lecturer. That is why it offers a theoretical discussion of the key issues together with real-to-life case studies. Hopefully, what has resulted will prove of interest to anyone involved in teaching students in higher education and those staff and educational specialists who increasingly facilitate the learning and development of academics. As I will seek to demonstrate, there are ethical responsibilities that go to the heart of what it means to teach with integrity in the modern university. It is essential that engagement with these ethical issues, and the responsibilities they imply, plays a core rather than peripheral role in defining professionalism in university teaching and as a focus for improving the quality of teaching and learning in higher education.

Part 1

The professional and ethical context

Chapter 1

The pedagogic gap

Introduction

University lecturers[1] are often involved in preparing students for the demands of professional life. This includes the education of future doctors, nurses, engineers, architects, lawyers and school teachers. Hence, it is somewhat ironic that lecturers working in universities have not traditionally been regarded as a distinct profession in their own right. University lecturers, though, have rarely presented an image of a unified and coherent professional group. They are commonly characterized as a disparate community of subject specialists or rival 'tribes' (Becher and Trowler, 2001), an insular image of strife within ivory towers that has been well recorded over more than two centuries (eg Kant, 1979).

These so-called 'tribal' tensions exist because for many teachers working in higher education their first point of identity is their discipline rather than their vocation as a lecturer. Others already possess a professional identity when they enter academic life as, for example, a lawyer, engineer, clinical psychologist, music therapist or medical practitioner. This professional or disciplinary identity provides many individuals working in higher education with their main external point of reference. In consequence, they will subscribe to this group's norms and values (Becher and Kogan, 1992). Many regard themselves,

---

1. The term 'university teachers' will be used interchangeably with other terms such as 'academics', 'lecturers' and 'professors' to describe staff with responsibility for teaching in higher education. This incorporates part-time and casual lecturers and postgraduate teaching assistants.

first and foremost, as researchers or experts in a disciplinary or professional field rather than *teachers* of their subject (Piper, 1992). This is also due, at least in part, to the role of the doctorate as the conventional entry route into academic life. By this means, young academics have been inducted into the traditions of a discipline through a research apprenticeship rather than the multifarious demands that will be placed on them as teachers of university students.

Possessing a doctorate has long been regarded as the only necessary qualification for someone to teach in higher education. In this way, to paraphrase Lee Shulman, the expert learner is instantly converted into the novice teacher. Although the logic may seem strange, it has long been presumed that scholarly expertise alone is sufficient preparation to enable someone to teach effectively in higher education. It is in these narrow terms that professionalism among university teachers has conventionally been defined.

A problematic concept

The concept of professionalism, though, is problematic for university teachers for other reasons. Notions of professionalism encompass both mastery of an area of knowledge and skill, and service beneficial to the client (Jarvis, 1983). However, academics have always been very wary of terms like 'customer' or 'client' (Gordon, 1997). Indeed, radical academics regard the use of such terms in contemporary higher education as symptomatic of a de-skilling process. Ritzer (1998), among others, has labelled this process the 'McDonaldization' of higher education, recasting the lecturer in the role of a service worker.

Hence, whether academics teaching in universities constitute a profession is a moot point. Indeed, in many ways academics are a more divided, disparate and less powerful group than they used to be. The conditions of modern higher education mean that institutions are employing growing numbers of part-time and temporary staff on insecure, short-term contracts (Ainley, 1994; Nelson and Watt, 1999). Moreover, a sharper division of labour exists among contemporary academics with many now employed, for example, in a 'teaching-only' or 'research-only' capacity. This division is a symbol of the pressures brought to bear by separate funding arrangements for teaching and research in public systems of higher education, such as the UK and Australia. These forces are contributing towards what Nixon (1996) terms a crisis of professional self-identity. They also suggest that, in some respects, university teachers are becoming even further removed from the conditions necessary to establish a coherent professional identity.

However, the changes that are occurring in higher education across many parts of the globe are also helping to shape a new professional identity for university lecturers. The expansion of vocational and professional courses in universities means that a doctorate is no longer the normal starting point for every academic career. Teachers in fields such as business and management, social work, education and nursing are more likely to have professional or vocational expertise rather than a doctorate. Indeed, more practically oriented professional doctorates in management, education and the health sciences are increasing in popularity, taken after, rather than before, career experience is gained. While some staff from vocational and professional backgrounds may wish to pursue research objectives, others may experience the pressure to conduct research and publish as alienating and unhelpful to their career ambitions.

Furthermore, university lecturers from vocational fields bring with them values from their various professions. Among these values is a commitment to the needs of 'clients' or 'customers' and less discomfort in applying this language to their own students. In turn, this concern to meet the needs of the 'end-user' makes many lecturers from professional fields attuned to the needs of the student as the direct recipient of a university education, while prepared to acknowledge the expectations of stakeholders such as employers and professional organizations.

The impact of massification

It is the expansion of higher education, though, that has probably provided the biggest impetus towards the development of a new sense of academic professionalism. The massification of higher education provision is a global phenomenon (Scott, 1995, 1998). It has occurred in many developed countries, including the UK, Australia, the United States and the Netherlands. In the UK, changes in government policy led to the expansion of the participation rate in higher education from just 6 per cent in 1962 to around 15 per cent by the mid-1980s. A second, more rapid increase in student numbers occurred during the late 1980s and 1990s. At the time of writing, it is estimated that the participation rate in English higher education has risen to 43 per cent of those aged between 18 and 30 years old (DFES, 2003). The UK government's espoused target is a 50 per cent participation rate for everyone under the age of 30 by 2010. While this may seem a tall order, the participation rate in the UK is lower than in many comparable developed countries such as Australia, the Netherlands or Sweden. National definitions of what constitutes a 'higher education' differ, and much of the planned expansion in the UK will occur through growth in sub-degree provision (DFES, 2003), bringing it closer into line with notions of 'tertiary education' elsewhere.

The impact of massification has been felt throughout the higher education sector. It has brought about huge changes in the teaching and learning environment of university life. While the phenomenon has affected some popular, broadly vocational subjects more than others, the ripple effects have been felt across the sector. In particular, as we shall see later in this book, massification has brought into sharp focus a range of issues connected with the management of student learning.

Higher participation rates have meant greater diversity in the student body. University students are no longer a small, socially homogenous elite who are necessarily 'in love' with their subject. While a student of history might have a 'passion' for the subject (Booth, 1997), learners in vocational areas, like business and management, are likely to be more motivated by perceptions of relevance to career aspirations (Coates and Koerner, 1996). Many come to university with modest qualifications or limited previous academic study, with pragmatic, rather than idealistic, goals to better their job prospects or change their current career path. Modern university students are also more likely to be mature adults working full- or part-time in order to support their studies. Indeed, a majority of students in UK higher education are over the age of 25 (DFES, 2003). However, efforts to widen access to higher education are far from complete, with social class continuing to play a vital role in determining who goes to university. Students drawn from professional backgrounds are five times more likely to participate than their counterparts from unskilled social backgrounds (DFES, 2003). Despite these shortcomings, universities now contain a broader mix of students from different social, economic and cultural backgrounds than ever before. Although there is still some way to go, higher education is now regarded as the right of the many rather than the privilege of the elite few.

The new diversity of the student body, in, *inter alia*, age, ability, social background, culture, motivation and economic status, presents significant ethical challenges for teachers. In teaching, assessing and managing students this diversity has an impact. It is no longer good enough to treat students as an immature, homogenous group with identical educational backgrounds. One indication of the impact of diversity is the growing significance of student support centres and supplementary instruction schemes within universities, often focusing on the development of language and numeracy skills.

Rising student numbers have also prompted more use of group work together with peer and self-assessment. While there are sound educational reasons that justify these responses (Brindley and Scoffield, 1998), they are also pragmatically linked to the demands of teaching and assessing more students. As we shall see in later chapters, there are underlying tensions here linked to issues of justice for the individual student. In group work assessment, for example, research indicates that students are exercised about 'free-riders' or 'passengers' who fail to contribute sufficiently to collaborative assignments (eg Kennedy, 1997; Bourner, Hughes and Bourner, 2001). How this problem is managed is an ethical issue as much as a technical one.

Finally, the traditional role of the state as a benevolent benefactor has been replaced by national governments acting as a 'hands-on' customer (Scott, 1995). This has manifested itself in the UK via the work of the funding councils in auditing the quality of teaching and research. The audit of research quality is also a feature of the Australian higher education system. Similarly, students are now encouraged to think of themselves as consumers of educational services. The notion of professionalism in university teaching is being shaped by the emergence of this more service-oriented culture with the 'student-as-customer' (Scott, 1999) in an increasingly competitive, market-driven higher education system. This has created another pressure within universities for teaching staff to adopt a more professional approach to their practice.

Professional development

Despite the emergence of a mass higher education system, the academic community has still retained elite 'instincts' or 'habits' (Scott, 1995). One of these elite instincts has long been the notion that academics do not require development for their teaching role beyond the acquisition of a doctorate. This elitist instinct, though, is on the wane. In the UK, the recommendations of the Dearing report (NCIHE, 1997) have led to the rapid development of professional development programmes for lecturers at most UK universities. Many of these programmes have been shaped by the dominant notion of developing 'reflective practitioners' (Schon, 1983) and the philosophy of student-centred learning (eg Ramsden, 1992; Laurillard, 1993). It is somewhat ironic, though, that the widespread acceptance of 'student-centred' teaching methods has coincided with massification. The practical difficulties of responding to student needs on an individual basis pose a major challenge for lecturers in the context of rising numbers and a deteriorating staff–student ratio.

Many programmes in the UK have been explicitly designed to conform to the accreditation requirements of the Institute for Learning and Teaching in Higher Education (ILTHE), a professional body for teachers in higher education formed in 1999 as a result of a recommendation contained in the Dearing Report (NCIHE, 1997). The foundation of the ILTHE was preceded in the United States by the establishment of the Carnegie Academy for the Scholarship of Teaching and Learning in response to the work of Boyer (1990) and others on the scholarship of teaching and learning. The Carnegie Foundation, along with bodies such as the Society for Teaching and Learning in Higher Education in Canada, provides a forum for debate, research and dissemination of best pedagogic practice, with associated fellowship schemes to showcase the work of innovative and committed teachers. Although parallel schemes are now in place within many institutions to reward excellence in teaching, pedagogic research and curriculum innovation, kudos and recognition within the academic community are seen to lie elsewhere, in subject-based research. Crucially, academics still sense that their achievements in subject-based research, rather than teaching, are more influential in terms of career advancement (Gibbs, 2002). The culture of academic life in this respect will take a long time to change.

The erosion of autonomy

The right to exercise some degree of autonomy in their 'immediate work setting' is a key characteristic of a professional person (Laffin, 1986: 21). Traditionally, university lecturers have enjoyed a considerable degree of autonomy in the way in which they manage teaching and learning relationships with students in writing courses, setting assignments, grading academic work, granting extensions and generally taking a whole series of decisions affecting students both individually and as a group. This does not mean that this power of discretion has always been used wisely or responsibly. While the age of consumerism is now upon us, a more deferential culture preceded it where academics were unaccustomed to having their decisions challenged. Freedom to exercise untrammelled authority over students should not be confused with some sort of 'golden age' of academic life. It was not a panacea for all ills. It led, in some instances, to an arbitrariness of decision making and abuses of power.

On the other hand, the environment of contemporary academic life is increasingly rule-bound. Governments across the world now demand that national higher education systems provide 'value for money'. They act as customers rather than benefactors, with students (and their parents) increasingly adopting the same attitude. Accountability has become a key watchword in respect of stakeholders such as students, parents, employers and general taxpayers. Government agencies have been charged with exercising this more 'hands-on' responsibility for ensuring that higher education offers value for money. In the UK, the work of the Quality Assurance Agency for higher education, and professional bodies in many subject areas, means that neither teaching nor the curriculum is any longer the private preserve of 'academic rule' (Moodie, 1996).

The room for professional discretion and judgement has been slowly eroded by a range of interrelated changes in higher education. These include massification, consumerism, modularization of the curriculum, the casualization of academic labour, government control and 'new' managerialism. In this environment, complex ethical issues of teaching practice are subjected to reductionist forces, with universities producing increasingly detailed and defensive codes and regulations. Such an approach seeks to convert complex ethical issues of pedagogic practice into a simplified series of rules driven by an emphasis on standardized regulations. These rules are often created by senior academic, managerial and administrative staff rather than engaging frontline teaching staff who have a better understanding of the current operational reality. As a result, many new lecturers are being inducted into a culture that discourages the use of personal judgement in resolving ethical issues in teaching (Macfarlane, 2001).

The rule makers in academic life are now the managers rather than the academics. The creation of managed national competition between higher education institutions and the evolution of global competition between universities have brought about irrevocable changes in management styles within higher education. So-called 'new managerialism' is a phrase which has come to represent this radical shift (Dearlove, 1995). Academic management based on principles of consensus and collegiality has been largely replaced by centralized management teams involved in market-led decision making. According to some analysts, the experience of staff in higher education has become one of 'subjection' to 'untrammelled managerial power' (Winter, 1996: 71). The competitive position of the institution determines issues in relation to the curriculum, research and teaching. In consequence, new managerialism has had the effect of divesting academic faculties and departments of their decision-making authority while simultaneously placing more responsibility at a lower level for key responsibilities such as budgetary management. Since it is central to the competitive position of the university, the management of the student learning experience is no longer the sole preserve of academic departments.

The forces of massification have shaped new challenges to the traditional authority of academics and presented practical problems in managing ever-larger student numbers. A gradual erosion of the personal relationship between students and teaching staff has resulted. Tutors in an elite system were often assigned a small number of students as personal tutees and learners in many universities received one-to-one tutorial support as part of their education. These arrangements still exist in a small number of institutions but students in modern higher education are decreasingly likely to benefit from this kind of relationship with an academic. It is true that students are still often assigned personal tutors in most universities but the likelihood that this will result in a close teaching and pastoral relationship has, in many instances, been lost in practice.

The erosion of the personal tutorial relationship has had a profound effect on the way institutions and departments within universities and colleges respond to issues connected with managing students. Fewer students are now genuinely *known* by members of staff. Similarly, from a student perspective, fewer *know* their teachers as a result of the casualization of the academic labour force. Part-time and temporary staff, paid on an hourly rate, are simply less likely to be in a position to offer tutorial support to students. Providing support for students often demands personal commitment from the tutor beyond formal contractual obligations. The deterioration of contractual conditions has also eroded goodwill. Teaching staff are now less likely to be able to vouch for the character of students, know their strengths and weaknesses as learners or understand their personal problems. In short, massification and casualization have had a damaging effect on the teacher–student relationship. It has also made it harder to make judgements about students on the basis of knowledge of individuals and their personal circumstances.

Mass student numbers, together with the perceived need for more flexible learning to enhance student choice and flexibility of study, have led, in many universities, to so-called 'modularization' of the curriculum. This has commonly brought about a division of traditional courses stretching across the academic year into shorter units of study. The benefits associated with a modular curriculum include flexible credit accumulation, enabling individual students to tailor their course of study to meet personal and career aspirations. The downside of modularization is an erosion of coherence in the educational experience of the student. The course experience can end up as an 'aggregative' rather than an 'integrative' one (Raffe, 1994). Beyond this, there is a loss in the continuity of the educational relationship between students and teachers. Modules or units of study may last a matter of several weeks rather than a whole academic year, providing limited opportunity for either party to genuinely 'know' the other. The 'course' of study, whether biology, history or economics, also provides students with their basic source of self-identification (Berry, 1995). This source of belonging is threatened under systems of modularization which permit choice at the expense of coherence and relationship building.

From a purely pragmatic point of view these changes mean that decision making about issues connected with student behaviour, such as how to deal with cases of suspected cheating or assignment extension requests, is now subject to increasing bureaucratization. The prescription of rules governing a whole host of situations involving the management of student learning has proliferated. Modularization means that students can be studying across a range of subjects and departments within a university. Rules are needed to cope with this complexity but also often mean that teachers will build long-term academic relationships with fewer students. The erosion of the personal tutorial relationship means that the management of students no longer operates on the basis of trust. This has reached a point where it is now quite a common requirement for students citing the loss of a close relative as a reason why they require an extension for an assignment to produce a copy of a death certificate as evidence of such a claim.

The response to the challenge of massification has, in other words, been a defensive and quasi-legal one. It may also, partly, be attributable to the impact of consumerism in higher education and the more litigious environment this has created. The writing of references for students is an area that has been particularly affected in this respect. Given the heightened possibility of claims for libel and negligence that may arise from writing an inaccurate student reference it is understandable that most institutions now have strict rules that govern their authorship. Universities provide teaching staff with a series of rules on a whole host of activities that were formerly governed by their personal and academic judgement. One of the most important areas in this new rule-bound culture is in relation to extenuating circumstances for handing in assignments past their deadline date. This issue is a focus of one of the vignettes in a later case study (see Chapter 5).

However, it would be illusory to imagine that all academics are opposed to this new rule-bound culture. Many are supportive of the need to 'externalize' and depersonalize decision making in this way:

> There is not a situation or a contingency to do with the recruitment, enrolment, teaching, assessment and grading of students that has not happened somewhere within the university. As with the application of legal precedence, we are guided by others' judgements, others' prior experiences, and I can save hours of distressing argument with a student who misses yet another deadline by pointing out that 'printer failure' does not appear on the list of 'valid extenuating circumstances' for late submission and there is nothing I can do about it. In this respect, the university acts as a benign Cerberus – benign to us, that is – and why keep a dog and bark yourself?
>
> (Marsh, 2001: 14)

Here the university's rules are seen as offering benevolent protection from difficult decision-making dilemmas. The statement represents a readiness not just to acquiesce but to welcome the culture of control because it makes the lives of academics easier and less fraught with difficult decisions concerning students. This attitude is hardly surprising in circumstances where teachers are responsible for growing numbers of students without commensurate support. Ridding themselves of discretionary powers is also attractive to some teaching staff with other espoused priorities, such as their personal research. This is understandable given the emphasis placed in most universities and university systems on the importance of research in securing tenure and promotion. Moreover, in some higher education institutions, there is little expectation that university teachers will forge personal tutoring relationships with students.

There are, though, many more selfless justifications for welcoming the rule-bound culture. One is fairness. Balancing the principle of fairness to the student group with fairness to the individual is something that university lecturers have always been concerned about. Rules also play an essential role in promoting consistency in decision making, ensuring that where more than one student makes an identical request or commits an offence under relevantly similar circumstances, all are treated the same. However, the massification of higher education leading to increased group size has led, inexorably, to rules designed to protect the interests of the majority from the potential abuse of discretionary powers for the benefit of individuals. The risk is that genuine individual needs and differences can be overlooked in well-meaning attempts to maintain fairness to the majority. This is a difficult balance to achieve and something that will form an important point of debate in later chapters.

Further, it needs to be recognized that while the autonomy of teachers may have been eroded in recent years by system-wide social and economic change, lecturers still possess a considerable degree of *de facto* power over student lives. Assessment of student work is probably the most obvious example. The power of assessment places university teachers in a unique position to influence the class of degree a student receives and, often in consequence, their future career prospects. This is an onerous and not always welcome challenge. The commonplace delegation of this task to graduate teaching assistants, in some institutional settings, is indicative of how unwelcome a professional responsibility assessment is perceived to be. Another example of the *de facto* power of lecturers is the way plagiarism is handled in practice. Research indicates that despite the plethora of regulations covering cheating behaviour, most incidents of plagiarism are dealt with informally by lecturers (Parry and Houghton, 1996). This may, in part, be due to the perception that university rules do not adequately reflect the complexity of cases and the different degrees of seriousness attached to a range of cheating offences (Franklyn-Stokes and

Newstead, 1995). Teachers may also be cautious of getting embroiled in a formal departmental or university case against a student.

Dealing fairly with assessment and plagiarism are just two examples of the ethical responsibilities of lecturers where, despite the development of a more rule-bound environment, they continue to exercise considerable autonomy. The issues are numerous and complex, with the power of assessment lying at the core of an essentially ambiguous relationship between teacher and student. Although the language of higher education may have moved on to emphasize the importance of student empowerment, independence and autonomy, a harsher reality still exists, sometimes uncomfortably, behind the rhetoric of this new lexicon.

The limits of reflective practice

It is ironic that the erosion of the autonomy of the university teacher has occurred at the same time as lecturers are being encouraged to engage in reflection about their own practice. Schon's (1983, 1987) notion of the 'reflective practitioner' has become firmly established as part of the vocabulary in fields such as teacher education (Reid and Parker, 1995) and nursing (United Kingdom Central Council for Nursing, Midwifery and Health Visiting, 1986) while serious interest exists among educators in other professions, such as accountancy (Velayutham and Perera, 1993). Schon argues that technical rationality is the dominant model of professional education which has the effect of driving out what he terms education for artistry. Calling for students to reflect on problems arising from a practical context, Schon emphasizes the primacy of using a practicum – or 'virtual' world – as a basis for students to reflect on.

The 'reflective practitioner' model has been hugely influential in the emerging field of educational and staff development for teachers in higher education. Indeed, in the UK, the ILTHE has adopted 'reflective practice' as a founding basis for their professional accreditation framework. Also, influenced by the UK Staff and Educational Development Association and the importance of this concept in teacher education for the compulsory sector, there has been a proliferation of courses on teaching and learning in higher education adopting reflective practice as a core principle.

However, 'reflection' tends to be conceptualized in terms of the technical specifics of teaching and assessment rather than the complex, associated processes of managing student learning. By definition, reflection is on 'practice' rather than broader contextual issues that shape the academics' role and determine their working conditions in relation to practice. It is no coincidence that courses in staff and educational development are often referred to as 'training'. They are too often about skills, processes and techniques rather than a critical evaluation of the challenges of academic practice. In other words, reflective practice is being deployed as a conceptual framework for preparing lecturers with the skills and knowledge needed to perform their (teaching) duties as 'competent' technicians rather than critical professionals. This justifies educational development as a narrowly conceived study *'for'* higher education rather than a richer and more context-laden understanding of what it means to be a university lecturer. The UK government's proposal for a set of national professional standards or 'competences' for teachers in higher education looks set to endorse this narrow conceptualization (DFES, 2003).

Further, while reflective practice may promote an ethos of continuous improvement, it is not safe to assume that academic staff necessarily enjoy the practical freedom to experiment with regard to teaching and assessment methods. The movement from an elite to a mass higher education system and the demands of quality assurance mean that many lecturers, especially in popular vocational subject areas, are now working as members of large course teams seeking to provide a consistent experience to many hundreds of students. The casualization of academic labour has also had an impact in reducing the autonomy of teachers with regard to reflective practice. While some casual staff are employed for their specialist expertise, there is now a growing army of poorly rewarded part-time lecturers with little job security or professional autonomy. Uniform lectures and ancillary materials allow little space for experimentation and creative independence in the classroom. In practical terms this reduces reflective practice to little more than rhetoric given the conditions of a 'McUniversity' (Ritzer, 1998).

The pedagogic gap

Although the development of programmes in 'teaching and learning' is indicative of a gradual move towards professionalism, the curricula of such programmes do not tend to address the wider professional role and identity of university lecturers. Despite calls for a broader vision for academic staff development, including an understanding of the higher education system (Blackstone, 1998), internationally, these 'training' programmes appear to conform to a similar format (eg Keeson *et al*, 1996), giving restricted attention to the broader social and ethical framework within which higher education professionals operate.

While the notion of reflective practice is clearly an important basis for educational development, there is a danger that other, broader aspects of professional education may be given insufficient attention. As I have argued, the concept of reflective practice has been used to support a fairly narrowly conceived study *'for'* higher education. By contrast, a study *'about'* higher education is concerned with the broader canvas of professional life. It gives attention to the philosophical, economic, social, political and managerial context of higher education.

A study 'about' higher education invokes issues less likely to be confined to the immediate environment of the lecture hall or the seminar room but equally as important to professional life. Studying the aims of a higher education, the reasons and consequences of restructuring, system and global change, organizational issues connected with the management of institutions, the meanings of 'quality' and quality enhancement, disciplinary and community values, such as academic freedom, and the responsibilities of the sector in terms of social justice are all examples of issues that might play a more prominent role in any rounded professional education of university staff. Moreover, this is not just a case of special pleading. Gaining a theoretical understanding of the purposes of a university education is essential to inform the practical task of curriculum design or, on a smaller scale, planning the aims of a teaching session. Indeed, without an understanding of the aims of a higher education, how is it possible to fully conceptualize aims and objectives in one's own discipline?

The relatively narrow focus of courses in academic development for university teachers is symptomatic of a gap between the theory of teaching and learning and the demands of professional practice. Few such programmes pay substantive attention to the broader aspects of academic practice such as curriculum design, the implications of system-wide change or the relationship between teaching and research. Teaching and learning programmes also reinforce the teaching–research dichotomy by implying that while academics require development for their teaching role, they do not need any assistance in honing their research skills (Rowland *et al*, 1998).

There is a growing and substantial literature concerned with pedagogic issues in higher education focusing on teaching, learning, assessment, evaluation and reflective practice (eg Brown and Glasner, 1999; Habeshaw, Habeshaw and Gibbs, 1992; Race, 1998). Much of this literature advocates innovative approaches to teaching in higher education via, for example, group work, peer assessment and computer assisted learning. However, there is a surprising dearth of literature concerned with managing the ethical implications of teaching in modern higher education. In a sense, there is a 'pedagogic gap' (Malcolm and Zukas, 2001) between the 'teaching and learning' literature and work that focuses on the social, economic, political and ethical context in which universities operate. This gap has contributed to a 'surface learning' about the nature of teaching itself (Rowland, 1999).

Teaching in higher education is not simply about mastering a set of skills or techniques for giving lectures, stimulating discussion or assessing student group projects. The demands of professional practice involve a much broader set of concerns. They cannot all be neatly resolved by adopting a particular 'tip' or technique. They involve recognizing and dealing with problematic ethical issues as part of managing student learning. Coping with this more complex reality is not reducible to an intellectually undemanding set of skills or competencies. Technical competence is only one of the attributes of professionalism. As Knight (2002) argues, there is more to teaching than the mastery of content knowledge and pedagogic technique. It is also about getting in touch with one's own values and the emotional drives that lie behind these attitudes.

Within most professions the concept of service results in an ongoing discussion of ethical issues as they impact on practice. It also results in the incorporation of ethics as a key component within professional programmes of learning with an attendant intellectual debate (eg Bridgstock, 1996; Brockett, 1997; Fleming, 1995; Van der Vorst, 1998). Moreover, this phenomenon is not confined to the 'ideal type' professions of law and medicine (Eraut, 1994). It also includes business professions such as accountancy, an occupation rarely associated in the popular imagination with a commitment to ethics (Cummins, 1999). Thus, a concern for ethics is a defining characteristic of almost every profession (Morris, 1995). Sadly though, the 'professional competency' approach to educational development (D'Andrea and Gosling, 2001) has become the dominant policy of UK universities. This approach tends to exclude a substantive considera-tion of ethics in teaching as 'relevant' to 'competency'.

Finally, while many universities have now established programmes in teaching and learning for their teaching staff, several of these are organized and taught by non-academic staff from a human resource management background. The education and development of teach-ing staff in higher education by individuals with no direct experience of this context are symbolic of the narrow way in which university professionalism is being conceptualized. This reinforces the false impression that 'effective' teaching in higher education is about mastering a set of decontextualized communication and managerial skills and processes. It is ironic that while most higher education lecturers are committed to developing higher-level critical thinking among their students (Barnett, 1990; Goodlad, 1997; Nixon, 1996), this quality is not thought to be necessary in becoming a good university teacher.

An ethical dimension

A study of the ethical aspects of university teaching is part of a broader conception of professional development and the particular concern of this book is to encourage the debate about the ethics of teaching in higher education. However, much attention, in the field of academic ethics, has traditionally focused on an essentially self-regarding agenda. This is largely wrapped up in research issues such as the falsi-fication of research data, the misuse of research funds or plagiarism by academic research staff. Academic freedom (for staff rather than students), institutional governance, tenure decisions affecting staff in US universities in particular, and power relations within the univer-sity are also part of this self-regarding agenda (see, for example, Evans, Ferris and Thompson, 1998, Whicker and Kronenfeld, 1994 or Kennedy, 1997). More generic organizational matters, such as inter-personal (eg sexual harassment or discrimination) and organizational abuse (eg equipment theft or 'padding' expense accounts), are also a key focus. While issues such as harassment or discrimination against some staff are clearly important, they do not represent ethical problems unique to universities and tend to focus largely on staff relations rather than staff–student relations.

A good example of this 'self-regarding' agenda is the literature and debate connected with academic freedom. As Donald Kennedy (1997) has pointed out, academics have focused a lot of energy and intellectual interest on the concept of academic freedom rather than academic duty. When it is discussed, academic freedom tends to be seen as something principally conferred on academic staff rather than students. This impression is reinforced by the prominence given to section 202(2) of the UK Education Reform Act of 1988 which defines freedom for academics as: 'Freedom within the law to question and test received wisdom and to put forward new ideas and controversial and unpopular opinions, without placing themselves in jeopardy of losing their jobs' (Education Reform Act 1988, section 202(2)).

Conrad Russell's book *Academic Freedom* (1993), for example, approaches the notion of academic freedom almost exclusively from the perspective of academic staff. Although it is rarely given explicit attention, it is clear that academic freedom is intended to extend to the student body. Among the values which the Dearing report (NCIHE, 1997: 79) identifies as being 'shared throughout higher education', and notably with students, is freedom of thought and expression. Academic freedom has been defined, in this more inclusive sense, as: 'The principle which gives both students and faculty in the classroom the right to say whatever they believe is pertinent to the subject at hand' (Nelson and Watt, 1999: 22).

Since academic staff *and* students are members of the academic community engaged in intellectual and independent enquiry, it follows that the claims of academic freedom should be taken to apply to both groups equally. In this respect the 19th-century German principle of *Lernfreiheit* adds another dimension to our understanding of academic freedom. This principle refers to the freedom of students to study where they choose and to be free to inquire and debate (Moodie, 1996). Barnett (1990) calls for the notion of student academic freedom to be more than an empty slogan and identifies negative and positive aspects of learner rights. Among the rights of the student identified by Barnett are voluntary participation and what is referred to as 'intellectual space' for students to evaluate the prevailing theories of the subject.

Hence, the protection of the academic freedom of students is one, if not the first, academic duty of teachers in higher education. However, while this entitlement is traditionally associated with freedom for academics to express opinions, regardless of their popularity, academic freedom must be meaningfully extended to the student body. Eric Ashby (1969) sums up the requisite 'attitude' of the university teacher as 'to teach in such a way that the pupil learns the discipline of dissent' (Ashby, 1969: 64). This is similar to MacIntyre's (1990) contention that a university should encourage 'constrained disagreement' in which the central responsibility of the teacher is to initiate students into conflict which is tolerant of everything except intolerance itself. Here, though, it is important that the actions of academic staff in their close association with particular theories, creeds, philosophies and attitudes do not unintentionally undermine student freedom of expression, an issue which is debated in greater depth in later chapters.

Conclusion

This book aims to help the process of bridging the 'pedagogic gap' between the professional competency approach to academic development and the ethical complexities of teaching and managing students. It will also help to fill a gap in the literature concerned with ethics and values in higher education that, as I have argued, rarely includes a substantive focus on practical issues of managing student learning. Further, in debating ethics and values academics have tended to focus more on their own self-regarding rights and interests rather than their responsibilities in relation to students as fellow members of the academic community. This too is an imbalance that needs redressing.

Further, the ethical responsibilities of lecturers in higher education cannot be considered in isolation from important contextual forces, mainly stemming from massification, which have increased the importance of academic professionalism within higher education. At the same time, the approach which universities are adopting to this need is, in effect, a deficit skills training focused on a narrow definition of 'teaching' rather than a fuller appreciation of professional or academic practice. The result has been a neglect of ethics in university teaching and an even more worrying conversion of complex ethical issues into simplified rules and procedures. Where substantive attention to ethical issues has occurred, this has often been conceptualized in narrow, policy-led terms, such as widening participation to meet espoused national and regional objectives.

This is why it is essential that lecturers debate professionalism in higher education in terms of the ethical responsibilities that they possess rather than limiting discussion to more narrowly technical aspects of 'best practice'. This debate is central to formulating a more 'grown-up' definition of professionalism. If we are genuinely to address our professional duties in relation to university teaching it is necessary to adopt a more rounded approach to the development of academic teaching staff.

Chapter 2

The lost dimension[1]

Introduction

The traditional authority of academics teaching in higher education stems from their disciplinary and professional subject expertise. They were historians, mathematicians, structural engineers, radiographers and sociologists before they became higher education teachers. A large proportion will possess doctorates in their discipline and will be actively engaged in adding to the sum of research, or challenging its precepts, in their field. Accordingly, academics are organized in research centres, departments or schools of study in universities in line with these disciplinary interests. As Padfield has argued: 'Academics love their subjects, otherwise they would not persist in academia' (Rowland *et al*, 1998: 139). However, while their authority and self-image stem from their subject expertise, the principal occupational identity of most is as teachers (Piper, 1992) and the increasing division of labour among academics means that some are being cast almost exclusively in a teaching role within mass systems of higher education (Nixon, 1996).

It is hardly surprising, therefore, that when asked to teach at university the main concern of most academics is, first and foremost, to focus on disciplinary knowledge, to pass on the torch of their subject to a new generation. They want to produce critical thinkers (Barnett, 1990) and get students to think for themselves (Nixon, 1996) about the discipline in which they are being inducted. Indeed, developing in

1. The title of this chapter is taken from *Education – the lost dimension* by Roy Niblett (1955).

students a capacity to think critically is, according to the US-based Carnegie Commission (1973), one of the central functions of universities. However, employment-related skills such as working with others, quantitative literacy and being able to use information technology have become increasingly important within contemporary higher education. Pressure from government, employers, professional organizations and research bodies now means that, in the UK and elsewhere, courses must explicitly identify how skills are being developed. Moreover, many lecturers, in vocational areas of the curriculum in particular, are aware of the importance of equipping their students with effective skills in preparation for the demands of the workplace and professional practice.

While it is now widely recognized that a higher education must develop students with both subject knowledge and skills for the workplace, the role of values remains a neglected or largely lost dimension of the curriculum. Drawing on Bloom's taxonomy of educational objectives, Bligh, Thomas and McNay (1999) identify cognitive objectives, adaptable occupational skills and affective objectives as the three key aims of a higher education benefiting both individual students and the wider community. Affective objectives include the development of attitudes, values, emotional integrity and interpersonal skills in students benefiting society via its cultural development. Indeed, the National Committee of Inquiry into Higher Education (NCIHE, 1997) in the UK identified the 'shaping of a democratic, civilized, inclusive society' (1997: 72) as one of the principal aims of a university education. However, these words have subsequently received little attention in practice in the context of the UK's quality assurance system with its emphasis on subject knowledge and skills development. An example of this oversight is so-called 'programme specifications' which UK universities are now required to produce for all major degree courses. These are intended as a succinct description of the aims, teaching methods and learning objectives of a programme of study and should be written in a way accessible to key stakeholders such as students, employers and professional associations. In guidance sent out by the UK Quality Assurance Agency for higher education, reflecting the advice given in recommendation 21 of the Dearing report (NCIHE, 1997), it is notable that the word 'values' appears just once, and quite tangentially, to emboldened and repeated advice on the inclusion of 'knowledge' and various categories of 'skills'. This example is symptomatic of the way in which values and affective aims are being quietly airbrushed out of the curriculum of higher education. Values are rapidly turning into a 'lost dimension' (Niblett, 1955).

Teaching through values

Developing a sense of common values is the glue that holds society together. Values are also essential to teaching in higher education. Misconceptions about the role of values in a higher education context contribute to their neglect. One of the biggest barriers is the perception among some teachers that values are tangential, or worse, irrelevant to their subject area. Lecturers sometimes argue that developing and discussing values is more appropriately left to individuals, families or religious groups. It is not, in other words, *their* responsibility. Part of the discomfort that some lecturers express is that they associate talk of 'values' with 'preaching' to students. Values, however, are relevant to all disciplines and do not necessitate religious convictions or a missionary zeal.

One example of this is the centrality of intellectual integrity as the cornerstone of academic life. All students on entering university, regardless of their field of study, are given the sternest of warnings about the evils of plagiarism, representing, as it does, intellectual theft of someone else's ideas. Many courses now require students to sign undertakings when they commence their studies or on submission of an assignment testifying that the academic work they produce will be or is their own. While this represents a bureaucratic response to the widespread problem of plagiarism (Walker, 1998), it signifies the centrality of intellectual integrity as a core value in higher education. While breaches of this value are sadly commonplace, the importance in which it is still held is significant and special.

A second example is seeking the truth, one of a cluster of aims, values and general ideas identified by Ronald Barnett in relation to higher education (Barnett, 1990). Seeking the truth is a central principle of research and in teaching terms demands that learners are assiduous and conscientious in unearthing and using sources of information. When a student produces a major piece of work with a very limited bibliography it is commonplace for a teacher to punish this shortcoming with a lower grade than might otherwise have been awarded. The rationale for punishing the assignment with a low mark is clear. It is because this represents not only a technical failure on the part of the student to use sufficient sources of information adequately but also a neglect of their academic responsibility to seek out the truth through a sufficiently rigorous evaluation of the relevant literature.

A final example of a value central to academic life is tolerance of others. This ensures that students in higher education are able to participate actively in 'a neutral and open forum for debate' (Barnett, 1990: 8). A preparedness to tolerate the views of others while respecting differences between individuals on the basis of gender, sexuality, class, race and so on is essential to the promotion of an atmosphere free of fear and prejudice. It goes to the heart of the need for academic freedom for students. In practical terms, classroom discussion would be impossible without tolerance and mutual respect.

Intellectual integrity, seeking the truth and tolerance of others are expectations that teachers in higher education have of their students. They are in no sense subject-specific or demand that lecturers preach about values. Thus, teaching does not necessarily have to be explicitly *about* values. Rather, teaching *through* values means that certain principles and norms of behaviour are embedded into our expectations of students and, crucially, our own practice. Imparting values is, in fact, unavoidable in the nature of teaching itself (Carbone, 1987).

Here, the importance of the teacher as a role model (Kennedy, 1997; Ottewill, 2001) cannot be underestimated. Many of the things students complain about, such as cancelled classes, inaccessible tutors and timetable clashes, can be indicators of a lack of professionalism (Ottewill, 2001). As the Robbins report on higher education points out, 'an ounce of example is worth a pound of exhortation' (1963: 181). Once again, this is particularly apposite with regard to the problem of plagiarism, about which all students routinely receive written and often verbal warnings. Yet, all this exhortation by academic staff is often undermined by lectures (and lecture notes) which fail adequately to reference key sources on which they draw. The lesson is simple. We should practise what we preach.

Differences of emphasis

Any discussion with regard to the responsibilities of university teachers leads us naturally to a discussion of the values that underpin teaching in higher education. Despite the clear-cut importance of ethics in relation to professional practice, values have received relatively scant attention in emerging definitions of professionalism in higher education. The word 'professional' is, in fact, more readily associated with teaching in the compulsory education sector, which is, in part, due to greater historical regulation of teachers in compulsory education.

It might be argued that values in teaching are universal in nature. They apply, in other words, as much to teachers in the compulsory sector as to those working in universities and colleges. Indeed, in many respects one would expect a range of common values, such as due process, equity, privacy, intellectual honesty, freedom of expression and the exercise of legitimate authority (Strike, 1990) to be of relevance to all teachers. In common with Strike (1990), Tomlinson and Little (2000) produce a code of ethical principles for the school teaching profession. However, as they point out, university teachers face additional dilemmas. Unlike teachers in schools, university lecturers are not acting *in loco parentis*. Generally, students in higher education systems are not legally defined as children and their teachers do not assume the same responsibilities as parents. One effect of this difference is that this places a greater onus of responsibility on students for their own actions while, at the same time, building in higher expectations with respect to confidentiality in, for example, keeping records of academic progress confidential. In practical terms it means that university teachers do not normally discuss the academic progress of students with parents. Increasingly, though, parents are seen as one of the 'stakeholders' of modern higher education. This means that some parents may perceive that they have a right to an explanation about the progress of their son or daughter, especially if they are now paying substantial tuition fees.

Another significant difference between teaching in the school system and teaching in universities concerns the power of assessment. Universities, by definition, award their own degrees. Universities set their own examinations and this means that lecturers commonly act as teachers and final arbiters of the examination performance of their own students. There is clearly an in-built tension here between the desire to encourage and motivate students to learn and the responsibility to sit in judgement on their performance (Shils, 1982; Kennedy, 1997). This tension is especially acute given the impact assessment decisions can have on the career prospects of individual students.

Thirdly, unlike teachers in compulsory education, many university lecturers conduct research and publish as part of their professional role as academics. This dual teacher–researcher role can create a difficult dilemma for university lecturers torn between a desire to carry out research in their field and the time-consuming nature of teaching preparation and supporting student learning via assessment, feedback and tutoring. Although much has been written about the potential synergy between teaching and research and the need for teaching in higher education to be research-informed, there are also tensions, especially when the teaching responsibilities of an academic do not closely match his or her research interests. The conditions of mass higher education make this increasingly likely, creating a potential cognitive dissonance between the lecturer's teaching duties and research goals. Moreover, in the UK and Australian context, university lecturers have come under increasing pressure in recent years to research and publish as a result of the Research Assessment Exercise (RAE) and Australian Research Quantum. Both are peer-reviewed audits of research excellence resulting in the grading of departments and the differential allocation of research funding from the government on the basis of this grading. This has created greater competitive pressures on institutions to improve their ratings and this, in turn, has had a significant impact on the expectations placed on staff.

Finally, it has been argued that the aims of higher education incorporate a special demand to encourage students to think critically and to get them to challenge propositional or professional knowledge (Barnett, 1990). If one accepts the logic of this argument, it places a higher degree of responsibility on lecturers to protect the academic freedom of students in university education if it is focused on the evaluation of knowledge rather than student acquisition of knowledge *per se*. Although one might expect to see relevantly similar values identified in relation to teachers in either higher education or the compulsory school sector, there are clearly crucial differences of emphasis.

Identifying professional values

The responsibility for identifying values for teachers in higher education rests, formally, with established and emergent professional bodies, both generic to teaching and specific to different disciplinary communities. Most formal programmes of development for academic staff in the UK are accredited by the Staff and Educational Development Association (SEDA) and/or the more recently established Institute for Learning and Teaching in Higher Education (ILTHE). As a professional body for higher education teachers based in

❏ **A commitment to scholarship in teaching, both generally and within their own subject**

❏ **Respect for individual learners and for their development and empowerment**

❏ **A commitment to the development of learning communities, including students, teachers and all those engaged in learning support**

❏ **A commitment to encouraging participation in higher education and to equality of educational opportunity**

❏ **A commitment to continued reflection and evaluation and consequent improvement of their own practice**

Source: Institute for Learning and Teaching in Higher Education

Figure 2.1

the UK, the ILTHE has identified five values which it expects all members to model in their behaviour, closely based on those previously adopted by SEDA (see Figure 2.1).

While the attempt to identify a set of values or professional principles is important, what is particularly noticeable about the statement produced by the ILTHE is its emphasis on the dominant notion of reflective practice and the social justice agenda, reflecting UK government priorities. It refers explicitly to equal opportunities and also alludes to the widening participation agenda. While clearly important, as I have argued, the social justice agenda goes only part of the way in explaining the duties of teachers in higher education. There is no explicit reference to the duty of protecting the academic freedom of students, for example, which Ashby (1969) and others have argued is central to the duties of university lecturers.

A broader approach is taken by the statement on professional ethics issued by the American Association of University Professors (www.aaup.org). The statement, a revised version of a declaration originally adopted in 1966, is organized on the basis of five paragraphs each addressing the responsibilities of professors in relation to a number of distinct domains: knowledge, teaching, colleagues, institution and community. The second paragraph of this statement is explicitly devoted to the duties of professors as teachers and incorporates expectations of professional conduct such as encouraging free pursuit of learning, respect for students as individuals, objectivity, non-discriminatory treatment and confidentiality. In relation to teaching, the statement makes clear that the first duty of professors is to 'encourage the free pursuit of learning in their students' and to protect their 'academic freedom'. Although more detailed in nature than the statement of the ILTHE, the key point is that this set of principles encourages the practitioner to act appropriately rather than prescribe an exact course of action for every circumstance. A similar, more detailed elaboration of professional principles is also provided by the Society for Teaching and Learning in Higher Education in Canada (www.tss.uoguelph.ca). This covers content competence, pedagogical competence, dealing with sensitive topics (see Chapter 4), student development, dual relationships with students (see Chapters 4 and 8), confidentiality, respect for colleagues (see Chapter 7), valid assessment of students (see Chapter 5) and respect for institution.

Compliance and integrity approaches

Ethical dilemmas do not, by their nature, lend themselves to simple solutions. Indeed, adopting a quasi-legal approach to ethics, based on a detailed code of practice, is unlikely to be the main means by which ethical behaviour among professionals is internalized (Strike, 1990). Unlike the legal or compulsory sector teaching professions, higher education teaching is not regulated or licensed, although in the UK most institutions now actively encourage lecturers to join the ILTHE. This is, perhaps, a *de facto* halfway house towards a regulatory approach that will be completed when national professional standards are imposed in 2004–5 (DFES, 2003). Rather, the ethical standards that are currently expected of lecturers are set out by university or college employers. More broadly, the behaviour of university lecturers is subject to peer regulation (Whicker and Kronenfeld, 1994). These factors make a detailed code of practice both inappropriate and impractical to enforce. Rather, it is important to establish and build on ethical principles and responsibilities. As we will see in Part B of this book, such principles can be readily identified by practitioners via discussion of appropriate case studies.

Here, an important distinction is emerging between general approaches to professional values or ethics. On the one hand, professional responsibilities are sometimes expressed in 'codes of practice' which can often be quite detailed in nature. Such codes, though, can quickly come to resemble little more than a rule-book to prevent unlawful or unethical conduct taking away the need for a lecturer to make a professional judgement in the process. The assumption at the heart of a detailed code of conduct is that professionals (or employees) cannot be trusted to act in the right way. Ethics that depend on detailed codes of rules and regulations are *restrictive* (Kjonstad and Willmott, 1995). They do nothing to engage professionals in a moral debate or get them to reflect critically about their practice. Indeed, prescriptive codes of practice take away a professional person's autonomy which, while never absolute, is essential to professional identity (Laffin, 1986: 21).

By contrast to this *restrictive* approach to ethics, there is an alternative *empowering* approach which may be adopted (Kjonstad and Willmott, 1995). Here, drawing on Kohlberg's theory of moral development, an emphasis is placed on what people should *be* rather than what they ought to *do*. In other words, an empowering approach might stress core values (like honesty or integrity) but not prescribe a particular course of action in any given circumstance. It is about moral growth of the individual and the development of their character rather than getting them to follow a bureaucratic set of rules.

In practical terms, an empowering approach involves identifying a set of core values or self-chosen standards. The principles identified by Nolan (1997) are a good example in this respect. Nolan's principles for conduct in public life do not prescribe a particular course of action but, rather, indicate the sort of character a good professional should possess. While an empowering approach does not provide a clear decision-making 'formula', it does encourage professionals to engage with ethical decision making in a meaningful way.

An empowering approach to professional values is essentially based on what has become known as virtue ethics, based on the teachings of Aristotle. More latterly, the work of Alistair MacIntyre (1981) has brought about a renaissance of interest in virtue theory which focuses on the need for the 'educated moral agent' (MacIntyre, 1981: 149) rather than a rule-based approach.

A virtue approach

As I have argued, massification has led universities and academic departments to introduce more prescriptive rules designed, at least in part, to ensure that the interests of the majority of students are protected. These prescriptive rules have also been imposed under the auspices of 'new managerialism' to ensure consistency in the operation of new curriculum structures. For example, rules on deadline dates for assignments are intended to protect the 'good' student who is working conscientiously by not giving an unfair advantage to other students who may be looking for a deadline extension to give them extra time to complete the task for no valid reason. The implicit justification for such rules here is that the overall well-being, or happiness, of the student body is being enhanced because they can work to the deadline safe in the knowledge that no individual is gaining an unfair time advantage. This type of reasoning is essentially *utilitarian* in nature. The rule is designed to maximize happiness (or minimize misery). What counts is the overall utility the group will derive from knowing that others are not gaining an unfair advantage, outweighing the difficulties and unhappiness that certain individuals might encounter in meeting the deadline date. The perhaps more acute unhappiness of a few individuals struggling to meet the deadline is less important, in effect, than the peace of mind that the group as a whole derives from knowing that the rule is in place. Their combined 'utility' is greater than the sum of the 'disutility' that the minority may suffer. The rules that now pervade many academic departments are based on this essentially utilitarian logic which concerns itself with the result or effect of a moral act rather than the moral act itself.

A different type of logic is provided by *Kantianism*. Utilitarianism is essentially concerned with the result of a moral act in producing the most utility (to maximize happiness or minimize misery) for *all* persons affected by an action. Kant (1964) argued that moral obligation is unconnected with consequences. His categorical imperative states that we should act only according to rules that we would be willing to see everyone follow. The logic of this 'universability' argument also implies that we should not treat people as means to an end since this is not something that we would wish people to do in relation to ourselves (the logic of reversibility). How, in other words, would you like it if someone did that (action) to you? The concept of reversibility is intuitively attractive as a means of determining the rightness of a course of action, in, for example, a lecturer putting her or himself in the position of the student, as the 'recipient' of his or her actions, when making key decisions. Being able to place oneself in the position of a student should not be too difficult for lecturers given that all academics were once, or perhaps still are, formally or informally, learners themselves. The notion of reversibility allows the impact of decisions on the individual to be thought through rather than generalizing about the overall impact of decisions using a utilitarian rationale.

However, both the utilitarian and Kantian approaches to ethics emphasize the importance of following a rational set of rules rather than engaging directly with our own character and judgement. In dealing with ethical problems people do not tend to sit down and decide to act as either a 'utilitarian' or a 'Kantian' (Solomon, 1992). They act on the basis of their character and 'gut' instincts. These decisions may well be informed by a concern to maximize happiness or judge the rightness of an act by reference to the logic of reversibility. In reality, though, a mixed bag consisting of our own personality, experience, emotions, religious convictions, family background and moral beliefs will underpin decisions we take in difficult or trying circumstances with often little time to reflect. Indeed, in many complex situations, the logic of utilitarianism and Kantianism appears to act in direct opposition. While we would wish to be sensitive to the individual who wants an extension for an assignment (and can remember our own experiences as students only too well), we are also concerned to make matters fair for the 'rule-abiding' majority of students. These competing 'voices' go to the heart of many such dilemmas in teaching.

The limitations of utilitarianism and Kantianism might appear to leave us in a jam. They determine the criteria for moral decision making, in terms of either consequences or (logical) duties, without getting us to draw on our own character (Pincoffs, 1986). Virtue ethics, though, provides an alternative approach. Derived from the application of Aristotle's work in identifying intellectual and moral virtues, 'virtue ethics' has been popularized in recent years by a number of philosophers, notably MacIntyre (1981). Unlike rule-based approaches, virtue ethics focuses on the character of the individual rather than the principles that govern the moral act itself. Virtues, quite simply, are the excellences of character that enable someone to achieve the 'good life' (Mintz, 1996). Moral virtues include justice, courage and honour, among others (see Figure 2.2).

At first glance this list of virtues may appear to be somewhat arcane. The terminology, in many cases, does not coincide with the language of contemporary life (Foot, 1978), but this does not mean that these virtues are irrelevant. Justice, which Aristotle contended was the most significant, is a case in point.

Furthermore, it needs to be understood that these virtues represent median points between extremes. A coward lacks courage, while

Courage	**Friendliness**
Temperance	**Truthfulness**
Liberality	**Wittiness**
Magnificence	**Shame**
Pride	**Justice**
Good Temper	**Honour**

Figure 2.2

having too much courage can result in reckless behaviour. It takes courage, though, to stand up for one's own beliefs and defend the rights of others. In modern usage, pride is often used as a quite critical, pejorative term: 'pride before a fall', 'he is too proud for his own good', and so on. It tends to be associated, in other words, with an over-inflated ego. However, pride, in a professional context, needs to be understood in more positive terms as pride in doing a good job, doing justice to oneself and serving one's community. Indeed, it is closely connected to the importance placed by emerging professional bodies for university teachers on the notion of 'scholarship'. This term is invariably connected with the expectation that professionals will at least stay up to date in their disciplinary field. It implies that we should not rest on our laurels but ensure that when we teach we have taken responsibility to ensure that the curriculum is informed by current thinking and recent research. It is about having pride in one's teaching rather than simply relying on last year's lecture notes and is underscored by Ottewill's (2001) plea for professionals to act as role models.

The relevance of Aristotle's list of moral virtues can also be seen in relation to modern attempts to identify sets of professional values. The Nolan Committee on Standards in Public Life (Nolan, 1997) was established in the UK as a result of a loss of confidence in the behaviour of public officials, notably politicians. It established a list of ethical principles (Figure 2.3) that focus firmly on expectations of character.

One of the criticisms of virtue ethics is that it assumes a certain level of agreement about the nature of virtues within a community. This criticism, though, indicates the particular relevance which virtue ethics has in respect of teaching in higher education or, indeed, for

Selflessness

Integrity

Accountability

Openness

Honesty

Leadership

Source: Nolan Committee on Standards in Public Life (First Report)

Figure 2.3

other professional groups. Universities are distinct communities of scholars consisting of both teachers *and* students.[2] Communities expect certain norms and standards of behaviour and universities have long been associated with the principles of self-governance. Despite the rise of so-called new managerialism (Dearlove, 1995), much of university life is still peer regulated (Whicker and Kronenfeld, 1994) and it is the nature of these peer-regulated norms that this book will seek to identify and disseminate.

Conclusion

Adopting a virtue ethics approach does not provide simple rules for ethical decision making. It does not prescribe a particular course of action for any given circumstance. It also assumes a certain level of agreement about the nature of virtues within the community. It is not the easy way out that some might prefer. Ethical dilemmas, though, are, by definition, complicated and rarely lend themselves to neat and easy solutions. There is no 'right' answer. However, there can be good professionals seeking to do their best in complex circumstances and exercising judgement on the basis of key principles. Making this 'good' judgement (or the intellectual virtue of *phronesis*, as Aristotle called it) is no easy task but possessing the autonomy to do so is essential to the nature of professionalism.

The chapters that follow in Part 2 of the book present some of the key ethical dilemmas faced by teachers in higher education. In the

---

2. This does not mean to imply that university communities do not also incorporate researchers, administrators and other support staff.

process they delve into a central and much discussed aspect of professional practice but one that is effectively a lost, or rarely acknowledged, dimension of life as a university lecturer.

Chapter 3

The case method

Introduction

The purpose of this book is to identify the moral virtues that teachers in higher education regard as central to their practice. In approaching this task, it was important to find a way of getting lecturers to talk openly about the ethical issues they face in a way that was based on real practice. At the same time, though, it was important to develop a method of investigation that did not put unfair pressure on subjects to share confidential or privileged information regarding their own students or colleagues. Moreover, in getting lecturers to talk about 'ethics', the process of articulation is also a challenging one. The language can appear intimidating and can lead to the obfuscation of meaning rather than its clarification. Indeed, ethics and values are not a subject that a lot of people find easy or necessarily comfortable to talk about. As argued in Chapter 2, explicitly broaching this subject can raise the hackles of those who negatively associate ethics with 'preaching' to students in a self-indulgent manner.

In short, it was important to find a method of investigation that would allow lecturers to discuss their principles unfettered by worries about confidentiality or articulation. At the heart of my argument, the 'ethics of teaching' is not about understanding a rarefied language or dealing with special circumstances. It is about identifying embedded moral virtues that enable individuals to deal with complex issues on a day-to-day basis. As this chapter will explain, a series of case studies were used as a means of exploring some of the key ethical issues of teaching practice.

The case study method

The 'case study' is a teaching method that has been widely exploited in professional education for well over a century. As an established pedagogic tradition, the case study method is closely associated with the teaching of law, business and management, and the medical sciences (Kreber, 2001). However, it is by no means confined to these disciplinary fields and is also strongly represented in engineering, geography and several other subject areas. The case study can be described as an approach to teaching which presents both fictionalized and factual accounts of life and events in a wide range of organizational and professional settings. It is 'a detailed description of a particular real life situation or problem as it happened in the past and could happen in the professional life of the student' (Kreber, 2001: 222). The use of a narrative account, building a sometimes exciting and gradually unfolding story, has the advantage of engaging student interest at a deeper level of learning (Roselle, 1996). Telling an interesting, concise story is only one element of a good case study. It should also be thought provoking, include central characters with whom students can empathize, lack answers which are patently clear cut and get students to think (Gross Davis, 1993).

The case study method consists of more than simply introducing students to case study material, giving examples in lectures or directing learners to particular readings. It is a pedagogic practice which is avowedly student-centred, with the teacher acting as the facilitator rather than the 'expert' (Grant, 1997). Students should take the lead role in interpreting and analysing the case study. Indeed, the case study is widely recognized as an effective means of getting students to apply theory to practice, or, at least, a simulated version of a practice environment. They stimulate students to learn experientially and are frequently used in conjunction with group work.

Case studies also fulfil another important pedagogic intention by allowing for the presentation of the curriculum in an integrated format. Students are encouraged, in the process, to understand the links between knowledge areas that are traditionally presented in separate disciplinary 'boxes'. This is an explicit objective of case studies in many fields, including engineering (Grant, 1997) and international business (Jensen, 2001). Integration is also a laudable objective for educational development courses in higher education that can enable participants to understand the interconnections between different aspects of academic practice, such as teaching, research and administration.

However, case studies are more than a value-neutral pedagogic tool for stimulating the interest of learners, testing their skills of application and enabling them to understand the links between knowledge areas. Case study design is indicative of the educator's underlying aims. One of the purposes of deploying a case study is to simulate a situation which might arise in a professional or work-related context and which places the learner in the role of a decision-taker such as a clinical practitioner or manager and then requires the resolution of this problem. The 'rightness' of the decision could then be both discussed and judged in relation to the known facts of the case. Here, the intention is to get learners to apply their theoretical or technical knowledge to a particular case or circumstance. At its simplest, this approach can take the form of basic vocational training in any applied field. In this approach, the teacher acts as the expert in determining how well the student has 'diagnosed' and sought to respond to the issue(s) raised by the case. By contrast with this rationale, the case study method can alternatively be deployed as a means of opening up discussion and debate about the complexity and nature of professional practice in any field. The use of case studies to illustrate the complexity and ambiguity of professional practice relates strongly to the work of Schon (1983). Here, the intention is to demonstrate what Schon referred to as the messiness of professional practice in a much broader social, economic, political and organizational context. In this style of case study, 'right' and 'wrong' answers are few and far between. Rather, the case study serves as a vehicle for getting students to make sense of theory and develop their own critical frameworks, with the teacher acting as a facilitator or co-inquirer within this process.

The distinction sketched out above between the use of case studies for focused vocational and broader educational purposes has been made by a number of writers across disciplinary fields (eg Barnes, Christensen and Hansen, 1994). These alternative philosophies have been labelled as the 'Case as Skills Development (or 'mode 1') and the 'Case as Conceptual Development' (or 'mode 2') (Booth *et al*, 2000; Rippin *et al*, 2002). While it is possible for case studies to fall squarely into either one of these camps, it is perhaps more instructive to think of this distinction as representing the end-points of a continuum.

Case study as research method

While the case study is widely deployed in management, social work, engineering, medical and legal education as a teaching tool, its potential as a research instrument is less well known. In particular, it is possible to deploy the case study as a tool for ethnographic research. Deriving from anthropology, ethnography involves drawing on socially acquired and shared knowledge to understand patterns of human activity. Often ethnography involves the researcher in becoming a member of the group he or she is studying for an extended period of time. Essentially, this involves participant observation as a data collection method in order to arrive at an understanding of the social world inhabited by members of the group under scrutiny.

Ethnographic accounts of lived experience are used predominantly, from a research perspective, to report and analyse observations as the end-point of enquiry. They provide an in-depth description of the phenomenon under study once understanding has been established by the researcher through observation. The position of the author of this book, though, is as an 'insider' of many years' standing within the group under investigation, namely the academic community. This means that case studies can be written from personal experience and observation as a precursor to research using the case studies as triggers for discussion and debate. Hence, this means that the case studies will be used as a research instrument to probe further into understanding the norms of the academic community.

The dilemmas chosen are designed to provide a context for discussing situations that involve an ethical dimension. Almost all of the case studies in this book reflect incidents which have happened to me or to colleagues of mine working in higher education. In this sense they are, like ethnographic novels and dramas, a product of a lived experience in a community and help to provide a means of understanding how an ethnic group is organized and relates to the wider world (Banks and Banks, 1998). Indeed, the world of higher education has its own rich strand of ethnographic fiction such as Kingsley Amis' *Lucky Jim* or Malcolm Bradbury's *The History Man*. However, this literature has had a tendency of over-representing accounts of life inside elite institutions, especially Oxford and Cambridge (Carter, 1990). By contrast, the case studies that follow are based in an imaginary institution which provides a mass rather than elite higher education experience. They purport to be what has been termed 'ethnographic fiction science' (Watson, 2000) by straddling the worlds of creative writing and social science. This has provided material which is 'made up' but 'true' (Watson, 2000).

Case studies and educational development

Nearly all universities and colleges in the UK now require their academic staff to undertake some form of formal staff or educational development. As a result, programmes in educational development for teachers in higher education have grown rapidly in recent years. However, as with any relatively new subject area in its infancy, there is a dearth of teaching material on which to draw. While there may be a number of well-established texts on teaching and learning in higher education (eg Fry, Ketteridge and Marshall, 1999), these, with very few exceptions, do not carry substantive case study material. This means, ironically, that while those facilitating the learning of lecturers on such programmes are routinely advocating the use of student-centred methods, such as problem-based learning, there is a shortage of palpable materials by which to demonstrate this ethos within educational development courses.

The case studies in this book arose, at least in part, out of a sense of personal frustration with the dearth of material available to teach the nature of academic practice to university lecturers on educational development programmes. They provide a means by which to plug this gap in the materials available to teach lecturers about the nature of academic practice. However, they were written with a particular purpose in mind. They are not designed to provide a vehicle for simulating simple problem-solving or decision-making tasks. In other words, they are intended principally as mode 2 rather than mode 1 case studies. As I have argued, the development of lecturers should not be regarded as an uncomplicated process of vocational skills training and the case studies are explicitly written in a manner that seeks to contest this conception of practice. Rather, the cases are deliberately complex and, in places, ambiguous. The fact that only part of the relevant information is present is a means of both aping reality and engaging participants in discussion and debate. The case study characters find themselves in few situations that are easily 'solvable'. While it is possible to make practical suggestions in tackling some of the symptoms of their predicaments, dealing with the causes is less straightforward. My purpose, then, is to get participants to think critically about the nature of their practice and how they can juggle the conflicting pressures that come to bear on their practice.

Part 2: a background

As I have argued, much of what is written about ethics in higher education is centred on self-regarding interpretations of academic freedom and social justice issues considered from a policy-level perspective. Despite the importance of these agendas, there is little practical focus on the day-to-day challenges that confront university teachers. This section seeks to address this need by use of fictional case studies.

Each of the chapters that follow is based around an exploration of a case study about a 'day in the life' of a fictional university lecturer. This consists of a series of incidents and decision-making dilemmas: incidents when teaching in class, receiving assignment extension requests, observing a colleague teach, responding to student complaints about colleagues and so on. Using case studies in this way as a mechanism for discussing moral virtues might be seen by some as an odd choice. This is because case studies have been subject to criticism as a pedagogic tool that tends to overly focus on 'quandaries' or 'dilemmas'. By doing so excessively, case studies can give an unbalanced impression of the nature of professional life, ignoring the positive aspects in favour of the less commonly occurring dramatic and emotional critical incident. Case studies in the teaching of applied and professional ethics are often illustrative of 'unethical' behaviour, by individuals and organizations, rather than stories of good people doing good things.

This criticism of 'quandary' case studies in ethics tends also to be associated with pushing learners into making choices on the basis of applying one of the rule-based approaches such as utilitarianism, Kantianism or, possibly, an atomized 'step-by-step' guide. One of the basic tenets of case study teaching is to get students to apply theory to practice and the use of case studies in the teaching of applied and professional ethics is a reflection of this goal. However, it is not my intention to use the case studies within this book for this purpose. As I argued in Chapter 2, rule-based ethical theories are 'reductive'; in other words, they tend to prescribe how to 'solve' a dilemma and deny the relevance of the character of the actor faced with the decision in the process (Pincoffs, 1986). The business of making wise choices when faced by dilemmas, though, is as pertinent to virtue ethics as it is to rule-based approaches.

However, there is no reason why case studies involving dilemmas cannot also provide a mechanism to discover more about the virtues which guide the actions of individuals. It is essential, though, that something is understood about the actor(s) in terms of character and working context. This is something that many simple, problem-oriented case studies tend to ignore. Knowing about the character and working context of individuals is a vital ingredient that exposes the poverty of adopting simplified and de-personalized rules in seeking to 'solve' case study problems. As such, the case studies in this book seek to provide the reader with at least some understanding of the character and working environment of the main protagonists. These brief sketches are important in understanding the problems faced by individuals in making difficult professional choices.

Just as there is no such thing as a typical 'day' in the life of a university lecturer, neither is there, of course, any such thing as a 'typical' university lecturer. There are many who make a teaching contribution, from senior professors to graduate teaching assistants and laboratory technicians. There are full-time, tenured staff and part-time lecturers paid on an hourly basis with no job security. Some are at the beginning of their academic career while others are well established or nearing retirement. Moreover, lecturers are drawn from a multitude of different social and educational backgrounds where gender, race, religion and nationality can mark important points of departure. Crucially, everyone has their own unique character and our decisions are shaped by this pot-pourri of personality, beliefs and social background.

Higher education lecturers work within a wide variety of institutional contexts, from elite universities with a global reputation for research through to community colleges with missions to serve local and regional needs. One university may teach mainly undergraduate students pursuing vocational courses while another may be focused on postgraduate education in the medical sciences. In some countries, such as the United States, there is a significant private sector in addition to public universities. Even within ostensibly 'unitary' systems of higher education, such as that in the UK, there are substantially different traditions (Scott, 1995). Indeed, the UK government has recently signalled its intention to encourage institutions to develop alternative 'missions' reinforcing existing divisions between research-intensive and teaching-intensive universities (DFES, 2003). In short, there is no such thing as a typical university. These differing institutional contexts mean that the conditions within which a 'university lecturer' works may vary starkly. This incorporates expectations in terms of teaching hours, departmental and faculty structures, 'service' work, opportunities for study leave and so on. Added to this, disciplinary traditions indicate marked contrasts with respect to teaching methods and grading practices, among other conventions. It would be impractical to represent all of these different traditions within a simple series of case studies.

The fictional institution represented in the case studies that follow is called 'The University of Broadlands', an institution founded in the 1960s as a vocationally oriented 'polytechnic' but which, since 1992, has been reclassified as a university. There is a student population of about 20,000 of whom 70 per cent are undergraduate students enrolled on a wide range of degree programmes in the Arts, Humanities, Health and Social Science. These contain a range of professional and vocational degrees in addition to more traditional subjects such as History and English. While this is a brief description, being overly prescriptive runs the risk of leaving readers feeling that they have little in common with the context. Nor is it, perhaps, a very imaginative or detailed institutional profile. Rather, it is broadly intended to be indicative of the environment of a 'typical' UK university in 2003. Given that two-thirds of universities in the UK were founded after 1960 (Scott, 1995), it is a characterization that, at the very least, is far from untypical.

The case studies I have produced do not seek to define 'the right answer' to any given moral dilemma but, rather, present a snapshot of the complexities that lecturers confront. The responses of lecturers to these case studies have been gathered in a wide variety of ways over the past three years. These include specially convened focus groups, *ad hoc* educational development events, conference workshops and individual correspondence with more than 20 of my academic colleagues. These individuals are representative of both sexes, a wide age range, differing levels of seniority, disciplinary traditions and institutional contexts. For coherence of presentation, the case studies are broken into a series of vignettes within each chapter in Part B. The responses to each case study are then reported, resulting in an interpretation of the principles and moral virtues that underpin the professional practice of teachers in higher education.

Conclusion

The case studies in this book serve a dual function: they can be used for both teaching and research purposes. As such, for readers who may prefer to consider using the case studies for educational development purposes, they are reproduced in unbroken form, without my commentary and analysis, in the appendix. As this chapter has explained, case studies have the potential to be deployed in different ways. Although I have focused on using the case studies to identify moral virtues in teaching, others may wish to deploy them with alternative uses in mind.

Above all, I hope readers will find these case studies authentic accounts of life as a university teacher. On the other hand, I trust that no one will take offence from the use of named characters. They are all figments of my imagination and do not refer to any individual lecturer, living or dead. In other respects I have tried to make the case studies as true to contemporary university life as I can. While perhaps not all of the events that occur represent the ethical dilemmas of a 'typical' day, they are intended to provide examples of challenges that many lecturers face at some point in their teaching career.

Part 2

Professional practice

Chapter 4

Teaching

Introduction

The word 'teaching' means very different things to different people. In higher education it is still, sadly, often interpreted in the narrow sense of giving a formal lecture to students. This tends to consist of a monologue, perhaps with elements of audiovisual illustration, rather than a dialogue. In lectures the lecturer does the talking and the students do the listening and note taking. There are, of course, ways of making the lecture more interactive (Bligh, 1998; Horgan, 1999). Essentially, however, lectures are largely about the performance of the teacher or 'lecturer' rather than about the learning of the students. This is more than a pedantic point. It represents an assumption about what constitutes 'good' teaching which fails to take full account of the impact on student learning. It has led to a strong emphasis on peer observation of lectures as a means of evaluating teaching practice (see Chapter 6) and is also reflected in the traditional assumption that the aim of teaching is to transfer expert knowledge from the teacher to the student.

While debating the characteristics of effective higher education teaching is not central to the purpose of this book, the lecture is symbolic of the power and authority of the lecturer and assigns an essentially passive role to the student. It provides the lecturer with a privileged platform for a variety of purposes from 'covering the curriculum' to being provocative. This latter purpose is about exercising the privilege of academic freedom. It is also connected to the goal of many educators to get students to think critically about knowledge. Ultimately, however, the lecture enables lecturers to assert their authority as an expert in their field and cultivate the respect of their students in the process. The lecturer is the 'sage on the stage' who is assigned the role of principal actor with the students playing an invisible or, at best, peripheral role (Kolitch and Dean, 1999). The lecture is a platform, in other words, which confers immense power on lecturers and brings with it a corresponding duty to give students space to breathe and develop their own critical voice. This is just one of the many ethical challenges faced by higher education teachers.

Giving a lecture, of course, is only one form of teaching and, as research has shown, not necessarily the most effective. There are many other forms of teaching such as facilitating discussion with groups of students, both in a traditional classroom and online, through problem-based assignments, laboratory experiments, providing one-to-one tuition and so on. In this chapter, the word 'teaching' is intended to refer to this broader definition of teaching in higher education. Teaching can range from anything from addressing several hundred students in a formal lecture hall to supervising a student on a work placement. Contexts vary immensely and it would be impossible to capture the variety and complexity of these numerous scenarios in a single book, let alone a single chapter. However, this chapter will seek to unwrap a few of the common ethical dilemmas to which teaching in higher education can give rise.

What goes on in the confines of the classroom has been likened by a number of writers and politicians to a 'secret garden' (eg Whicker and Kronenfeld, 1994). Indeed, it is only in comparatively recent years that this 'secret garden' has been visited by government inspectors and the occasional colleague working on some form of peer review process (see Chapter 6). While this is not true of all subject areas in higher education, where lecturers have traditionally worked closely with colleagues in the classroom as part of a team, it is a characteristic of much university teaching. One of the inadvertent effects of the growth of online learning platforms, such as WebCT and Blackboard, is the way they are bringing more openness to the way in which lecturers teach. Web sites and online learning platforms provide a window on the changing world of teaching in higher education.

The secret garden metaphor is important in other ways. It also signifies that teaching is a deeply personal and emotionally demanding activity. It requires a 'monumental investment of self' (Seldin, 1993: A40). Societal expectations mean that the act of teaching is not generally positively associated with the language of love. Indeed, love is a taboo word in connection with the classroom (Hooks, 1994). Despite this, the intensity of the teaching relationship has led a number of academics to talk about the teaching relationship as one of love. Rowland (2000) explores the mismatch between increasing emphasis on bureaucratic and centralized notions of quality and the teacher's love of the subject. Freire (1997) speaks of both love of others and for the process of teaching itself. The flip side of investing so much of one's emotional self into the teaching relationship, however, is the bruising impact criticism can have through student evaluation (see Chapter 6). While teaching induces a sense of emotional vulnerability for some academics, it needs to be recognized that students are even more likely to be sensitive to criticism and will, in some cases, be relatively emotionally immature. Hence, there is vulnerability on both sides of the teaching relationship.

Teaching dilemmas

The case study that appears below is intended to capture some of the ethical challenges that lecturers face in their teaching role. The difficulties facing the lecturer will be revealed gradually through the chapter, with analysis and commentary following each vignette. This format will be repeated in subsequent chapters through this section of the book. The analysis represents a summary of that provided by my various 'respondents' – from focus groups, conference workshops and individuals – mediated by my own commentary and occasional references to relevant literature.

The awkward silence

Dr Lesley Chung has worked as an Economics lecturer at The University of Broadlands for the past 10 years. She went part-time for 18 months three years ago after starting a family, but recently returned to a full-time position at the university. Lesley was previously employed at a neighbouring university as a research assistant where she completed her doctorate in environmental economics. Subsequently, although she has sustained a keen interest in social and environmental analysis within economics, she has found it increasingly difficult to keep up her research and publications. The demands of teaching and administration, coupled with responsibilities as the primary carer for her young son, have made it difficult for her to find the time to publish, although the Head of Economics sees research as 'the department's number one priority'. Her work mainly consists of teaching Economics to first-year undergraduates.

Lesley's teaching commitments include a number of regular weekly seminars in first-year Economics to groups of between 15 and 20 students and tutorials to individual students. She also teaches her own specialist module in Environmental Economics to second-year students, depending on demand. Seminars are used within the department to follow up on lectures, with an emphasis on student-led analysis and discussion. Thinking back over what happened during today's seminar, Lesley does not feel entirely happy. Two incidents occurred which are now worrying her.

The first incident happened close to the start of the seminar session. The students had seemed to be in good humour, perhaps because the end of term was drawing near. As usual, she had spent the first 10 minutes or so of the seminar recapping on some of the key concepts discussed the previous week. Lesley found this a useful way of checking that the students had done sufficient reading and worked through exercises in the course text following the lecture. It was also a two-way process where students could ask Lesley to clarify concepts they were unclear about. There was a light-hearted atmosphere at the start of the seminar and it became clear to Lesley that not enough work had been done in preparation for today's class. After a series of unsatisfactory answers to questions, one student made a particularly inept response at which point Lesley said, sarcastically, 'Clearly you've left your brain at home today! Can anyone else provide a meaningful answer to the question?' There was a ripple of laughter followed by an awkward silence. After a few seconds one of the brighter students in the seminar answered the question in a satisfactory way and the discussion moved on.

Lecturers frequently complain that students fail to participate enough in class activities and discussion. 'I asked a question in the lecture and not one of them put up their hand!' is an all too common cry of exasperation. This can partly be attributable to a lack of active learning techniques. Students, for example, can be given the opportunity to ask or answer questions in small groups before being exposed to individual questioning. Instead, all too often, students are asked to take a personal risk in front of a large peer group. Here, it is important to recognize that speaking in class is, crucially, a matter of psychological safety. From a student perspective, in other words, is it worth the risk? Making an oral contribution that is either incorrect, or simply poorly received by the tutor, can expose a student to embarrassment or, at worst, a sense of utter humiliation. A potentially even more damaging consequence might be loss of the good opinion of peers. Perversely, this can result from appearing to be 'too clever', as well as simply getting the answer wrong, given the existence of social pressures on both male and female students.

It is very easy inadvertently to crush the fragile confidence of a student of any age through a casual aside or failure to act on a crucial occasion, such as the one faced by Lesley Chung. Moreover, to criticize the student's thinking in such a dismissive manner is a hurtful thing to do and threatens his or her ego (de Bono, 1976). Without creating an atmosphere of trust where the lecturer can be relied on to protect the individual student, it is very unlikely that any class will develop into the kind of learning environment where the full possibilities of intellectual criticism and debate can take place. Tolerance and mutual respect are important ingredients for any educational experience based on democratic principles (Freire, 1997).

Hence, teaching, like many other activities, is about developing a relationship with other people, often over a relatively short but intensive period.

Almost all my respondents were critical of Lesley for making the off-the-cuff remark that 'clearly you've left your brain at home today' and referred to the importance of building a trusting relationship with the class. Many also felt that her remark represented an abuse of power. While Lesley may be rightly disappointed by the level of student preparation, personalizing her comments in this way is likely to damage a relationship where trust is central. If she had wanted to express her sense of disappointment, she could have avoided personal criticism and the use of sarcasm by chastising the group's performance as a whole. Assuming that Lesley hopes to promote the continued active involvement of her students, she needs to consider the likely effect of making such a personal remark. This effect, according to some respondents, might well be to put a permanent end to the willing and active engagement of this student in class. Moreover, the 'ripple effect' of this putdown creates a sense of fear that could potentially end the future participation of several other students in the group.

Several respondents pointed out that students take a great personal risk when making an oral contribution. Even if they know the answer to a question they may prefer to stay silent. For students, the approval of their peer group may be more important than that of the teacher. By getting a question wrong, let alone being chastised, they might perceive that they are losing a lot more than the good opinion of the lecturer. It is easy enough to bruise the confidence of a learner without trying, let alone crushing the ego of a student in such a deliberate and public manner. Using sarcasm and putdowns is a violation of what is sometimes termed 'interactional fairness' (Rodabaugh, 1996).

There was common agreement that Lesley should make an apology to the student, in a public way in front of the class. Although Lesley may perceive this initially as a loss of face, it is vital if she is to re-establish trust with the group. Here, the notion of respect for learners was cited as a key underlying principle. According to this view, Lesley cannot hope to create a classroom environment based on mutual respect if she is incapable of modelling this attitude herself. While apologizing in private at the end of the class might undo some of the damage, it was generally agreed that being prepared to retract the remark in front of the other students would be the most appropriate and effective way forward.

It is easy, though, to be critical of Lesley's action in this case. Which teacher can honestly claim never to have made a remark in class they regret at some stage of their career? A small number of my respondents pointed out that Lesley's sharp putdown was prompted by a proper and sincere concern that the students were paying insufficient attention to their work. Although her remark was inappropriate, it was prompted by understandable emotions. Lesley has taken the failure of her students to prepare adequately as a personal affront and her outburst was prompted by her commitment as a teacher to get learners to take their reciprocal responsibilities seriously. It is important, respondents commented, for lecturers to be demanding in this way without allowing this exacting attitude to get out of control, as in this instance.

The 'lively' debate

Lesley believes passionately that economics should not be taught as an abstract science that ignores social and environmental issues. In today's seminar she had arranged for a structured discussion of government 'macroeconomic' priorities on the basis of two articles and a short video shown to the group. At first this stimulus material had worked well, leading to a lively debate with a series of good points being made, including the interdependence of national economies. Unfortunately, an incident occurred during discussion, which is now causing Lesley to ponder. She had tried to draw out one of the quieter students, called Sam, who had previously been too shy, it had seemed to Lesley, to make an oral contribution in class. Things got heated, though, when he had said, 'Friedman's right. Getting inflation down is much more important than unemployment. That will sort itself out in the long run.' However, this remark resulted in a terse and angry retort from another student, called Jane: 'Extremists like you make me sick. You wouldn't say that if your father had been unemployed for the past 8 years.' The sharpness of this exchange took everyone by surprise, but after an uncomfortable silence of a second or two the discussion exploded back into life, with several students contributing in rapid succession, although Sam did not take part. The difficult moment had passed but Lesley was left wondering then and again later, on reflection, whether she should have intervened at this point. She had hesitated to intervene at the time, she recalled, because she sensed from Jane's terse reply that she was speaking about how unemployment had affected her own father. Perhaps she had also not intervened because Lesley felt broadly supportive of Jane's view. She was not sure whether she had done the right thing to say nothing or let the incident go as part of the general 'cut and thrust' of classroom debate.

There is a difficult balance that needs to be struck here. On the one hand, lecturers want to challenge, question and make students uncomfortable about their taken-for-granted assumptions about knowledge and the world in general. They want to make them into critical thinkers. On the other hand, in creating this creative chaos and taking students out of an intellectual comfort zone, it is important to establish a clear, stable and supportive environment in which this enquiry can take place. Brookfield describes this challenge for teachers as walking an 'uneasy tightrope' (1987: 73). He argues that while risk taking is central to the critical thinking process, this behaviour is unlikely to occur unless those involved have no sense of fear. It is crucial that this psychological contract between the lecturer and the student is supported if critical thinking is to be effectively promoted as part of the teaching process.

Lesley is clearly committed to trying to stimulate critical thinking in her class by selecting a controversy for discussion. However, for there to be a productive and positive atmosphere of investigation and reflection, it is essential that she fulfils her responsibilities as part of the implicit psychological contract. Here this consists of the need to ensure that debate takes place in an environment free from intimidation and where full respect is demonstrated for different perspectives on the issue. In this context, her failure to protect Sam is a violation of this psychological contract. Creating a 'neutral and open forum for debate' is an important component of the value background of higher education described by Barnett (1990: 8). Establishing this kind of environment is easier said than done in practice. For this forum to be genuinely open, students need to feel that their contribution will be valued and that the environment created is genuinely one based on trust and mutual respect (Sachs, 2000).

Many of the respondents spoke again of the importance of the principle of respect both in terms of the lecturer's need to respect her students and the importance of students showing respect for the views of their peers. Our treatment of others should not deny their basic humanity and dignity. This is the point made by Kant and explained in terms of the second formulation of the categorical imperative. The fact that as human beings we want to be treated with respect means that it is only rational for us to treat others in the same way. The logic of this argument is powerful and provides a useful way of explaining to students the fundamental need for respect as a core principle underpinning all learning relationships.

With regard to the vignette, most of my respondents agreed that Lesley should have intervened immediately after the sharp exchange that took place between Sam and Jane. At stake here were important principles connected with freedom to express ideas and opinions on the part of students while demonstrating a respect for the views and personal experiences of others. Many commented that it is essential to establish firm 'ground rules' protecting and promoting a tolerant atmosphere for discussion. The danger of not intervening in this situation is in the signal it might send out to students about the risks of contributing to discussion. According to some of my respondents, students can be fearful to contribute because they are aware of the fact that they hold opinions that might be deemed unpopular or unfashionable. By not intervening, Lesley would merely reinforce this fear, while taking action would have the opposite effect.

Respondents suggested a range of practical techniques for group discussion which might have avoided the bitter exchange between Sam and Jane in the first place. Several of these ideas involved allowing students more preparatory time to discuss the issue in pairs or small groups as a means of 'siphoning out' extreme or ill-considered views and reactions. It would also allow more time and space for establishing mutual understanding of different personal perspectives in a safer environment for the exchange of ideas. One or two respondents argued that Lesley should have used the heated exchange between Sam and Jane as an opportunity to give students 'time out' in small groups to reflect on the issues in an arena less 'public' than that of the whole group debate.

The vignette raised wider issues with regard to the responsibilities of lecturers who deploy active and experiential learning methods. While such methods have gained popularity as a means of improving student learning and connecting with their opinions and real-life experiences, it is also essential to be prepared to deal with the consequences of deliberately or unintentionally provoking an emotional response. Quite simply, when encouraging participation there is a greater chance of the unexpected happening. Here, respondents recognized the need for lecturers to possess what has sometimes been referred to as 'emotional intelligence' (Goleman, 1995). Demonstrating empathy with individuals making personal statements, such as Jane's, while also acknowledging and valuing Sam's view, is important in this context. Failure to deal effectively and fairly with this kind of incident is likely to damage the relationship between the group and the teacher. While some respondents were of the view that 'emotion' should have no place in student learning through discussion, the overwhelming majority regarded engaging students in this way as important to their social and intellectual development.

The incident also highlights the fact that Lesley's intellectual sympathies lie with Jane rather than Sam. We are also told that Lesley is committed passionately to an interpretation of her discipline that places a strong emphasis on the social and environmental effects of economic activity, such as unemployment. Whether this lecturer's strong views are known to the student group is left unexplained. However, for some respondents this was also a key issue. If she had communicated her strong intellectual beliefs in uncompromising terms to the group this might, according to these respondents, have had the potential to undermine trust in her as a fair arbitrator in classroom discussion. Those holding alternative views to Lesley's may feel intimidated to contribute to discussion unless they felt sufficiently reassured that they would receive fair treatment by her conduct. A different point of view is that it might be intellectually dishonest for

Lesley to keep her convictions hidden from the group. Teaching is not a value-neutral activity and communicating a passion or enthusiasm for a subject is generally regarded highly by students as contributing to the quality of their learning experience. There is an important dilemma here for any lecturer, although one that is rarely discussed. Regardless of where one might stand on this issue, the essential point coming out of this vignette is that students must be able to trust their lecturer to provide them with a safe environment in which to discuss and debate. The views of individuals need to be treated with respect both by the lecturer and by each other.

The persistent tutee

While thinking about the incidents in class earlier in the day, there was a knock at her office door. It was Brian Stevens, yet again. He had been to see Lesley at least three or four times recently about a final coursework essay due in next week for the Economics course. While Lesley had made it clear to the class as a whole that they were welcome to see her for a tutorial about their essays, as usual, few had taken her up on the offer. This had been a relief in a way given her workload and problems sharing an office with a colleague. However, Brian had seen her for an initial discussion about sources, a second time to talk through the essay titles and on two further occasions with different essay plans. He was a bright and conscientious student who had done well in his previous assignments but basically seemed to lack self-confidence. This time he had brought along an essay draft and asked whether Lesley could have a quick look at it to let him know whether he was 'going in the right direction'. To Lesley, it looked more like a near-completed essay than a 'draft'. It came as a welcome relief when the telephone rang, giving Lesley the opportunity to ask Brian to return during her next scheduled 'office hour' the following day. She was in a quandary, though, about what to do about Brian's request as he was bound to return tomorrow.

The principal issue for respondents in dealing with this dilemma is the need to preserve the principle of fairness or equity. By spending so much time advising Brian Stevens on his essay their concern is that the help he is receiving is disproportionate to that received by other students. Hence, most respondents saw this dilemma in terms of the need for teachers to apportion their time fairly between students because of *perceptions* of fairness even if, in reality, Lesley is largely providing Brian with emotional reassurance rather than additional academic help. Others regarded the dilemma as about fair apportionment of academic assistance between students rather than time *per se*, although arguably this could amount to much the same thing in practice.

Despite these considerations, it is not easy for Lesley to send Brian away in a perfunctory manner simply on the grounds that it would be 'unfair to the other students'. The difficulty facing Lesley in this situation is that she also has a responsibility to Brian as an apparently academically (and possibly emotionally) insecure individual. He clearly wants (or needs) reassurance more than anything else. Hence, there is a need to be sensitive to Brian's character and circumstances and deal with him on a compassionate basis.

His requests for constant tutorial support may mask more serious personal difficulties and even, as one or two respondents suggested, a romantic interest in Lesley. This raises an important issue about the boundaries between professional and personal relationships. While this vignette does not directly set out to explore so-called 'dual' relationships, where a sexual and/or romantic relationship may exist or be developing between a student and a teacher, it at least needs to be acknowledged that the tutorial relationship provides the most likely context for the unfolding of this type of scenario. Here, the student and the tutor are meeting in private and without the social inhibitions attached to the management of a classroom. Lesley needs to take care that her actions are not open to misinterpretation. If she should feel uncomfortable about the unfolding situation it might be advisable to meet Brian in the presence of other colleagues or ask him to seek help from another tutor in future. The issue of dual relationships will be explored in more detail later in the book (see Chapter 8).

Rather than focusing on the issue of fairness to other students, a number of respondents analysed the scenario in terms of the responsibility of Lesley, as the lecturer, for developing Brian as a more confident and independent person. It would be for this reason, rather than fairness to others, that they would decline to give him any more assistance with the essay. According to this view, weaning Brian off too much tutorial help would be a step towards making him a more independent learner and ultimately help him grow as an individual.

The vignette illustrates the need for teachers to balance sensitivity to the needs of the individual with two other relevant considerations. One is the perception of favouritism among other students which could result from over-attentiveness and, at worst, speculation that she has entered into a dual relationship with Brian. The other is to ensure that her concern for his academic and pastoral welfare does not overwhelm Brian's need to develop more independence as a learner and self-confidence as an individual.

The unwelcome module

The telephone call had been from the Head of Department confirming the bad news that insufficient student numbers had opted for Lesley's Environmental Economics option in order for it to 'run' next term. Instead, to make up her teaching hours, Lesley would be expected to take the Economics of European Integration option. Lesley was disappointed about not being able to teach her specialist area and had mixed feelings about teaching the Economics of European Integration, an area she had little real interest in which drew heavily on international trade theory. While she had taught this option a few years ago, filling in for a colleague who had been on study leave, she felt pretty rusty in this specialist area. Looking at her notes, a little later in the day, she thought she had probably got enough to 'get by'. If she did not spend too long in preparing to teach the module she might even be able to finish a research paper which she had been trying to complete for more than 8 months now. Besides, she had heard a rumour that the department would be advertising for an international trade specialist for the beginning of the next academic year and probably he or she would take over the teaching of this option anyway from next academic year.

Lesley Chung is trapped by a conundrum that faces countless lecturers in modern higher education. Should she concentrate on her teaching or her research? Is it possible to do both without compromise? Given her other commitments, including being the primary carer for her child, it would seem that the answer is 'probably not'. Academic careers are still largely shaped by achievements in research rather than teaching. While what is perceived as teaching 'competence' may be important in tenure decisions in both North American universities and some institutions in the UK, such as Imperial College, progress up the career ladder after this point is perceived to depend more on research achievements rather than teaching excellence. Moreover, Lesley's Head of Department had made it clear that research should be the priority. It is obviously in Lesley's best interests, in pure career terms, to focus on finishing her research paper. The culture in which she finds herself working also puts pressure on her to publish.

Most of my respondents recognized the 'fix' Lesley found herself in here as a commonly occurring dilemma of academic life but were understandably reluctant in many cases to confront this issue head-on by suggesting one specific course of action. Many were in favour of Lesley trying to achieve both objectives: teaching the module well and finishing her paper by judicious time management. Others suggested that she should be more pragmatic: do enough to 'get by' teaching the module and concentrate on finishing her research paper which would more directly help to further her career.

Some respondents focused on the need for Lesley to redefine her own assumptions about what constitutes 'good' teaching. This does not necessarily imply just 'knowing the stuff'. It is also about getting the students to engage with the challenges of the curriculum and take responsibility for their own learning. Indeed, one or two respondents suggested that Lesley should 'come clean', tell the students that this is not her expert area and approach teaching the module in the spirit of a co-learner. According to this approach, Lesley should tackle this unwelcome teaching assignment in an open and honest way. This would produce a better learning experience for students than simply 'covering the ground' in a way that projects no enthusiasm on her part. Self-disclosure about one's lack of expertise was suggested both as a means of connecting more closely with students as learners and as a requirement of intellectual honesty.

At the heart of this particular dilemma is another rarely acknowledged truth about teaching in much of modern higher education. This is that the lecturer's expertise does not necessarily correspond with the specialist area they find themselves teaching. This is particularly the case for lecturers involved in teaching broad vocational subject areas, such as business and management, which comprise 'hard' and 'soft' knowledge from pure and applied contexts (Becher and Trowler, 2001). Teaching beyond the traditional confines of disciplinary expertise is also a consequence in many subject areas of mass student numbers without a corresponding increase in resources or staffing.

The economics of fluctuations in student numbers means that while students may perceive the lecturer to be the expert, the reality may be rather different. Very few respondents suggested that Lesley should refuse to teach the module. The expectation that teaching staff should be flexible is a common enough modern managerial requirement and one that was largely accepted as part of the lot of the modern lecturer. In contrast with the previous vignettes where power largely belonged to Lesley, here it appears to rest with her Head of Department who has placed her in this difficult situation.

Although a few respondents suggested that Lesley should concentrate on her research paper, most who confronted the issue directly argued that, faced with such a stark choice, she should prioritize the preparation of her teaching. For these lecturers, professional 'pride' or 'integrity' demanded that Lesley place the interests of her students before those of her own career goals and the espoused research priorities of the department. Here a strong sense of duty to students was conveyed in the comments of respondents. As discussed in Chapter 2, pride is often more popularly viewed as a vice rather than a virtue. It has negative associations with human failings such as arrogance and dogmatism. In this context, however, the notion of pride or 'professionalism' was articulated as a communal virtue since it was often explained as part of a desire to 'do one's job properly'. As one lecturer commented, 'Could Lesley live with herself if she didn't bother to prepare this course properly?' Ultimately, for these respondents, Lesley's first duty should be to her students in prioritizing preparation of course materials and updating her own knowledge base in the area.

Conclusion

Lesley faces a series of different and difficult challenges. She is concerned about her own somewhat terse remark at the beginning of the class during the question and answer session. She is worried about whether she should have intervened when a student made a heated and unpleasant response to another during the class discussion. She is wondering what to do about the student who keeps seeking tutorial guidance. Finally, Lesley is wondering how to use her energy in the months ahead with both teaching preparation and research goals in mind. Naturally, these are but a few of the dilemmas lecturers face in their daily lives as teachers. However, they begin to unravel the complexity of the teaching role and reveal some of the key values that underpin the practice of lecturers. These include establishing a teaching relationship based on trust, modelling and encouraging respect for others and caring for students while maintaining a reputation for being fair (or just) to all. In terms of the virtues that lecturers need to model, the case study highlights the importance of *respectfulness* in class interaction, *sensitivity* towards those that seek tutorial support and adequate preparation to teach as an aspect of professional *pride*.

The interplay between values and emotions was central to the analysis offered by my respondents. The importance of emotion as a legitimate component of ethics has long been neglected (Blum, 1980; Oakley, 1992). This is partly due to the dominance of 'rational' approaches to ethics such as Kantianism and utilitarianism. Emotions are regarded as the antithesis of a rational calculus. However, my respondents spoke often of the importance they attached to qualities such as empathy and compassion. These they regarded as important as more 'rational' qualities, such as respect for others or fairness. As Oakley (1992) suggests, emotional excesses may be morally bad. Establishing a happy medium between extremes of emotion such as passion for the subject as opposed to the disinterested pursuit of knowledge is vital. Lesley clearly cares about her discipline but losing one's temper is not a positive emotion. Similarly, Brian, the tutee, needs to be shown sympathy but not to the extent that this results in a lack of attention to Lesley's other students or in giving him disproportionate academic assistance.

More generally, this case study also illustrates that it is important not to 'box off' the teaching role too much. In other words, teaching issues are often shaped by the interplay between the other roles academics perform as researchers, personal tutors and members of an academic department. The wider policy and institutional context has an impact in shaping our priorities as teachers, most notably in relation to research. The interaction between teaching and the other roles academics play is a theme that will be explored further in the chapters that follow.

Chapter 5

Assessing

Introduction

One of the key differences between teaching in the school system and teaching in universities concerns the power of assessment. As discussed in Chapter 2, universities, by definition, have the power to award their own degrees. This places lecturers in the dual position of teacher and final arbiter of the examination performance of their own students. The responsibilities of this dual role are sometimes difficult and uncomfortable. While lecturers are motivated by a desire to nurture the academic and personal growth of their students, they must also act as a judge of their own success as teachers. There is clearly an in-built tension here between the desire to encourage and motivate students to learn and the responsibility to sit in judgement on their performance (Shils, 1982; Kennedy, 1997). The future career prospects of individual students can hinge on the judgements made by lecturers with whom they have developed a close academic and pastoral relationship over several years. While blind marking of student work is on the increase as a mechanism for eradicating bias in assessment, in practice lecturers are often aware of the identity of the student.

Hence, using their power in a wise and just manner is a key issue which concerns all educators (Kreisberg, 1992). Moreover, the credibility of new lecturers among students may depend on their ability to handle issues of perceived justice as much as the quality of their formal teaching. Rodabaugh (1996) comments that fairness is the most important factor identified by students in describing their 'best' teachers. Here, procedural matters are deemed more important in determining fairness than grades awarded (Rodabaugh and Kravitz, 1994). Indeed, evidence indicates that students rate fairness in assessment as a more important measure of teaching quality than anything other than teachers having expertise in their subject (Ledic, Rafajac and Kovac, 1999). The changing nature of contemporary higher education is also creating fresh challenges in assessment. The adoption of new forms of student assessment, such as group and peer marking, is an innovation that has significant implications for arbitrating fairly and acting in a manner where justice is transparent.

There is also a pragmatic case for paying greater attention to the exercise of academic power. Evidence is growing that students increasingly conceptualize their relationship with universities as a consumer of educational services (McKee and Belson, 1990; Ritzer, 1998). From an organizational perspective, this more litigious environment ought to necessitate a focus on the tight management of the rules of natural justice. It follows that a moral and practical understanding of fair assessment practices lies at the heart of the pedagogic role.

Clearly, therefore, there are substantive issues surrounding the way university teachers exercise their power and responsibility in relation to assessment. The move towards continuous assessment of learning in higher education has, if anything, increased the importance of setting fair assessments, granting extensions, adjudicating in disputes between students working in groups and in various other aspects of assessment management. Plagiarism is another key issue. Evidence suggests that this is increasing due to a range of factors, including more use of continuous assessment, Internet access for researching assignments and the adoption of an increasingly instrumental attitude by learners. This means that students act 'strategically' and put in the minimum effort for the maximum return. If something is not assessed, the strategic student (Kneale, 1997) will not bother to study that part of the curriculum or participate fully in the learning activity. This trend is linked to a broader range of contemporary trends in modern UK higher education such as massification, vocationalism, the changing age profile of students and the introduction of tuition fees. In addition to the implications of innovative pedagogy, these trends have also had an impact on shaping new ethical challenges for higher education teachers. Several of these are reflected in the case study presented and discussed in this chapter.

Assessment dilemmas

As one of my former colleagues once dryly observed, the assessment role can ruin a perfectly good relationship with a group of students. It is the part of the job that many academics dislike the most, both in terms of the workload involved and the need to make a judgement about the quality of student work. It is hardly surprising, therefore, that those with the least power and status as teachers in higher education, including doctoral students, graduate teaching assistants and junior lecturers, are often called upon to assist in the marking of undergraduate work.

The duty of academic staff to assess student work brings with it perhaps the most demanding set of ethical obligations. It also tends to be an area which is most heavily subject to university rules and procedures, although the power and individual discretion of lecturers should not be underestimated. The following case study, therefore, provides an interesting contrast in the approach adopted by lecturers to ethical issues connected with assessment while also illuminating important commonalities.

The group dispute

It is Dave Andrews' first term as a lecturer in Sports Science at The University of Broadlands and he has been finding it hard going. After spending most of his twenties doing a PhD and then working as a postgraduate research assistant on various projects, Dave secured a lectureship on a three-year contract last September. Although Dave did 'pick up the odd seminar' while working as a researcher, he started his new job with very little teaching experience. He was shocked that as a new lecturer he was given such a heavy teaching load and feels dumped with several irksome administrative jobs, such as 'quality assurance', which clearly no one else in the department wants to do.

Today, Dave has a busy day ahead with teaching in the morning and the afternoon. He desperately needs to finish marking some assignments which he has promised to return to the students by the end of the week. He also has a scheduled 'office hour' at lunchtime in order that students can come to see him on a first-come-first-served basis. Dave returns to his shared office after finishing his morning teaching. It is now his office hour but he decides he needs to get on with his marking.

Before he can get very far, though, there is a knock at the door and three students enter. They want to talk to him about a group presentation, an assessed part of their course, which they are due to do next week. Dave listens while the three students tell him that the fourth member of their group has hardly ever turned up for meetings to discuss the presentation and is generally not 'pulling his weight'. The students say they have done a lot of work and are worried that the fourth group member 'will just turn up and take equal credit for all our hard work' on the day of the presentation. On the other hand, they are also concerned that their grades will suffer as the fourth group member has not prepared properly. They ask whether they can do the presentation without the fourth member. Dave tells the students that he will have to think about it and sends them away with a promise to see them the next day.

Dave Andrews is an inexperienced, young lecturer who has been 'thrown in at the deep end'. He appears to have received little in the way of preparation for his role as a lecturer in higher education and needs to rely on his limited teaching experience as a former doctoral student. This experience, however, will probably not have equipped him for the kind of challenges he now faces. Sadly, as my respondents were quick to confirm, this is an all too common scenario in higher education. While doctoral students are sometimes required to help with the grading of assignments, it is less common for them to have experience in designing their own assessment tasks. A lack of clarity about the rules governing the group assignment and the lecturer's expectations may lie at the root of the problem he faces.

The student who is (allegedly) failing to 'pull his weight' is a phenomenon normally referred to in the literature as 'free-riding' or 'freeloading'. Evidence indicates that students find it is one of the things they like least about working in a group (Bourner, Hughes and Bourner, 2001). However, it is not an easy issue to deal with and raises important concerns about fairness to the individual. The view expressed by most lecturers, especially more experienced staff, was that the group should be told to sort the group problem out for themselves. The argument here was that working with others is part of the reality of life, especially in the workplace. This 'reality' is all about working with people you do not particularly like but making the best of such circumstances. The action favoured by these teachers would be to talk to the group, emphasize the workplace metaphor and not allow the students a 'get out' solution such as individual grades or 'dumping' the fourth member. Respondents who tended to favour this view were drawn not only from professional and vocational disciplines. They also included many from non-vocational fields who argued that making the students sort out the problem themselves was essential to getting them to understand the importance of taking responsibility for their own learning.

However, in balancing the advice that this issue should be defined as the students' problem rather than Dave's, most respondents also recommended that the 'ground rules' on completing this sort of group assignment should have been established at the outset. Here, a range of 'solutions' were suggested by respondents, all designed to build control devices into the group work process and ensure that justice is done in the process. Some of the solutions, such as peer assessment, may also have additional learning benefits for students by stressing the importance of assessing learning as a process. In dealing with the alleged free-riding problem a minority of respondents contended that Dave needed to find a means to seek evidence for each individual's contribution to the group assignment. A number of ideas and potential solutions were put forward (Figure 5.1).

Where a more interventionist stance was recommended, it was also pointed out that lecturers should investigate the facts of the situation clearly before rushing to any judgements. It is possible, for example, that a personality clash may have occurred between members of the group. How can we be sure, in other words, that the fourth member of the group is really a free-rider? It may be that the three members of the group forming the delegation have simply taken a dislike to, or

> ❑ **Establishing managerial roles and responsibilities within groups**
>
> ❑ **Requiring minutes of group meetings to be taken**
>
> ❑ **Allowing group members to peer assess each other's contribution to the assignment**
>
> ❑ **Assessing individual reflective learning logs on group processes**
>
> ❑ **Assessing individual components in group reports and other artefacts**
>
> ❑ **Allowing groups to 'dump' un-cooperative group members/ permitting an individual to complete a group assignment individually**

Figure 5.1

'frozen out', the fourth member. Indeed, illness or personal problems might lie behind the failure of the fourth student to turn up to student group meetings. Investigation to get at the truth is then clearly essential in a host of situations like this and is a fundamental professional responsibility before taking any significant action which may have the effect of penalizing the apparently errant fourth member.

An allied issue that became a focus of attention during discussions of this vignette is the process by which students are selected to form groups for assessed assignments. While some lecturers allow students to self-select, others prefer to engineer a grouping, often seeking to strike a balance within a group on the basis of factors like nationality, gender, age, learning style and so on. Also, groups are sometimes put together in a deliberate attempt to represent a range of ability levels, facilitating knowledge transfer between group members and creating an in-built support mechanism for weaker students in the process. However, while organizing groups in this way can produce learning benefits, it can also result in complaints from students who believe that their individual degree award may be adversely affected as a result of being teamed with 'weaker' peers. According to Whitley and Keith-Spiegel (2002), students have a preference to be graded on their individual contribution to group work. They argue that students are less likely to cheat if their grades match their own performance. Here there is a clear tension between the way higher education has moved towards greater use of group learning but maintained an award structure based on the reward of individual excellence. This is a conundrum which all teachers in higher education need to face up to rather than dismiss as an insignificant issue.

Two similar essays

Munching a sandwich, Dave returns to his marking but quickly becomes concerned about two essays which appear very similar. On closer inspection Dave notes that there are whole paragraphs which are almost identical save for the odd word or different phrase in places. He remembers that the two students had worked well together on an earlier group project and are probably good friends. Dave sighs and puts the two essays to one side. He will have to think about this.

Unfortunately, such a scenario is not uncommon in the assessment of student work. It is a problem that teachers in higher education will gain experience of sooner rather than later. Opportunities for plagiarism are on the increase (Walker, 1998), with greater emphasis on continuous assessment rather than terminal (ie end of course or module) examinations (Parry and Houghton, 1996). Student access to Internet sites with the attendant opportunity to download or 'copy and paste' large chunks of text is another factor. Greater use of group learning means that students are, on the one hand, being encouraged to work together more while, at the same time, still being required to produce individual pieces of work. This is, perhaps, sending out a mixed message which means that students perceive group learning as a means of facilitating and, on occasions, excusing plagiarism (Ashworth, Bannister and Thorne, 1997).

Despite the existence of detailed rules for dealing with cases of suspected plagiarism, though, the evidence suggests that lecturers mostly handle such incidents informally without recourse to central university guidelines (Parry and Houghton, 1996). Participants who took part in discussion about the incident of suspected plagiarism fell roughly into two camps. One group of participants emphasized the importance of following all aspects of institutional procedure in handling the case, while a second group focused more on how they would personally investigate the matter. This latter group of participants favoured finding an informal, 'negotiated' settlement with students rather than bringing in the 'big guns' of university procedures and committees of investigation. Collecting evidence and being sure of the facts were seen as vital by everyone offering procedural advice (see Figure 5.2).

A number of participants commented that plagiarism can sometimes be the result of student ignorance or inexperience, especially among those in their first year at university. Such students, for example, may be labouring under the false impression that in-text acknowledgement of a source is only necessary when they are quoting word for word. It was also commented that students from different cultures and educational systems can be schooled in the belief that education is about reproducing knowledge, rather than analysing or evaluating it, resulting in written work which deliberately plagiarizes sources. Students from South East Asia were mentioned in this context. In such circumstances, and where the plagiarism offence was relatively minor, some lecturers favoured an

❏   **Follow university and/or departmental procedures**

❏   **Collect the evidence and be sure of your facts**

❏   **Interview students you suspect of collaborating separately**

❏   **Ask colleagues for their opinion**

❏   **Be consistent in handling cases**

❏   **Be aware that student inexperience or ignorance may explain some forms of plagiarism**

❏   **Be aware of cultural differences in understanding what may be considered to constitute plagiarism**

Figure 5.2

informal approach with a correspondingly lenient punishment, such as a requirement to rewrite the essay or a minor reduction in the grade awarded.

To some extent, however, the reactions of participants to this incident were similar. Virtually no individual suggested taking personal responsibility for a formal investigation. Those who recommended following institutional procedures tended to see this as a means of passing on responsibility to someone else more senior than themselves, while those recommending an informal resolution were reluctant to take the incident through official channels. The reaction of this latter group of participants is in line with the findings of Parry and Houghton (1996) but contrasts with the expectations expressed by Whitley and Keith-Spiegel (2002). They contend that confronting, and dealing effectively with, cheating behaviour is a central academic obligation. Moreover, according to Whitley and Keith-Spiegel (2002), trying to explain why students may have cheated should not act as a rationalization for inaction.

The extension requests

Just as he is about to mark another essay, there is a knock at the door and a student enters looking somewhat sheepish. The student explains that he feels under a lot of pressure because he has a number of assignments due in at the same time. He also mentions that he had a cold last week. The long and the short of it is that he wants an extension on the essay set more than two months ago at the beginning of term. Realizing he is due to teach a class in a few minutes, Dave tells the student to come back in the morning to discuss the matter further.

After finishing his last teaching session, Dave returns to his office and remembers that he had better check his e-mail. Dave opens two messages from students. Opening the first e-mail, he recalls that this student is attentive and a good attender, although he is yet to mark any of her written work. The e-mail explains that as a dyslexic student she would like a few days' extension on the assignment deadline in order that it can be checked over for errors by an adviser at the Student Learning Centre (a central body at Broadlands which, among other things, helps students with learning difficulties). The other e-mail is from a mature student Dave teaches on a part-time postgraduate course. This student also wants an extension, citing 'work pressures'. Both of these requests for an extension relate to the assignment set more than two months ago at the beginning of term. Dave decides not to reply immediately to either e-mail in order to think over the requests before making a decision.

Extension requests bring the principle of fairness to the majority into direct conflict with fairness to the individual. Dealing with extension requests demands a difficult balancing act between these two imperatives. This central dilemma was recognized as a key challenge by participants who commented on the various scenarios presented in the vignette: the student with a lot of other assignments due who also claimed to have had a recent cold; the request of the dyslexic student for extra time to have her essay checked over by the Educational Support Unit; and the part-time, mature student who wants extra time to complete his or her assignment owing to 'work pressures'.

A number of lecturers, mainly, but not exclusively, teaching in vocational subject areas, emphasized that meeting deadlines is an important discipline for professional and business life. They were reluctant, therefore, to extend deadlines as a matter of principle since this would not reflect the 'realities' of the workplace. Hence, they regarded meeting deadlines as developing time management as a work-related skill. Potential (or current) employers of these students, it was argued, would not be prepared to accept excuses in failing to meet deadlines for the completion of work and lecturers would be failing in their duty of preparing students adequately if they treated them any differently.

These lecturers were particularly dismissive of the part-time mature student requesting an extension owing to 'work pressures'.

The use of this strict workplace metaphor was not shared by all who discussed the scenario. A number of participants commented that allowances need to be made for mature students with family responsibilities who may be acting as the primary carer of young children or elderly parents. The personal circumstances of the individual were, hence, important to take into account and were distinguishable from, say, a young undergraduate without similar responsibilities. The fact that many students in UK higher education now work on a full- or extensive part-time basis to support their studies led some lecturers to comment that more account needed to be taken of the extension requests of all students, regardless of their 'maturity'.

Respondents were generally most sympathetic to the extension request of the dyslexic student seeking additional time to have her assignment checked for grammatical errors by the support unit. This attitude, though, was far from universal. A large minority of respondents felt that the student's dyslexia was an inadequate excuse for seeking an extension given the fact that the assignment had been set more than two months ago. They would be disposed to dismiss the request owing to the student's unrelated inability to manage her own time effectively. Others were suspicious that the request represented a ruse to seek additional time to actually write the essay rather than have it checked over. Here, asking the student to show Dave a copy of the assignment as currently drafted before granting any extension was suggested as a practical means to ensure that the lecturer was not being 'conned' in this situation. However, in focus group discussion this suggestion was condemned by another respondent as a breach of

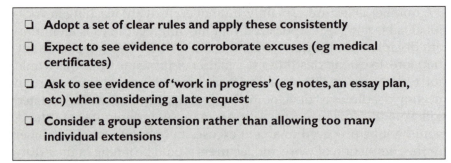

Figure 5.3

trust, especially given that this student is considered by Dave to be of good character.

In giving extensions there is an overriding concern to treat the group, as well as the individual, with a sense of justice or fairness. In this respect it was suggested that rather than giving too many extensions to individuals, it was preferable to extend a deadline to all students in a group to ensure that nobody could claim to have been disadvantaged or treated differently.

The gift

Half an hour later the departmental secretary appears at Dave's office with a gift for him left in the departmental office by a Chinese student from Hong Kong. The present, wrapped in Christmas paper, turns out to be a large (2 litre) bottle of whisky (Dave's favourite tipple is single malt and he remembers, somewhat guiltily, how he made some light-hearted reference to this effect, as an aside, at his last lecture). The card reads: 'To Mr Andrews, my favourite teacher, Merry Christmas and a Happy New Year, thank you for all your help, best wishes, Lee'. Dave recalls that this is a hard-working student but one who has struggled to gain good marks partly due to problems with written English. Ironically, Dave has Lee's latest assignment as the next one on the pile to mark. He wonders what he should do about the bottle of whisky.

Lecturers commented wryly that receiving gifts from students is a comparatively rare event as a university teacher! However, a number of respondents recognized that giving gifts to teachers is a common enough practice among students from South East Asia. This, though, should not necessarily be interpreted as a deliberate attempt to influence a grade or gain some sort of academic advantage. It was pointed out that this gift could be an innocent token of Lee's appreciation and respect for Dave. Cultural norms vary in relations between students and teachers and this fact should be taken into account in considering how to deal with the gift.

Hence, simply declining to accept the gift might cause offence. On the other hand, accepting it, under these circumstances, would, according to most respondents, compromise Dave's position of impartiality as an assessor. While simply receiving the gift may not of itself have any direct influence over Dave's ability to assess Lee's essay in an impartial way, he needs to consider how the situation may be perceived and interpreted by others. Here there is a parallel with perceptions of favouritism which arise in Lesley's tutorial relationship with Brian in Chapter 4.

Given the circumstance Dave finds himself in, respondents were agreed that his actions should be transparent. The fact that the gift is a bottle of alcohol also complicated the issue for some respondents who felt that discovery of such an item in Dave's room might lead to an assumption that he is in the habit of drinking at work. This could potentially lead to disciplinary action. Moreover, simply accepting the gift in private would lay Dave open to accusations of favouritism that might compromise him. Instead, it was suggested that he might be able to accept the gift, to share at a future departmental social function or to raffle for charity. These solutions were designed to ensure that Dave could not be accused of bias or favouritism.

Other respondents commented that Dave's position would be quite different if the gift had been offered either after the end of teaching a course when the assessment had already taken place or if the gift had been from a group of students rather than just one individual. In these circumstances Dave's impartiality as an assessor would not have been threatened in the same way. Receiving a gift at the end of teaching a course of studies may be interpreted less ambiguously as a 'thank you' rather than some sort of compromising inducement. Also, to accept a gift from a group of students does not carry the risk of implying favouritism to any one particular student.

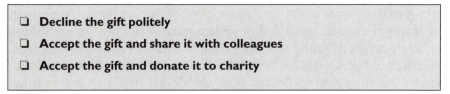

❏ **Decline the gift politely**
❏ **Accept the gift and share it with colleagues**
❏ **Accept the gift and donate it to charity**

Figure 5.4

Conclusion

In discussion of this case study the words 'fair' and 'just' cropped up time and again. Dealing with the various incidents in a fair and just manner was a core component of all the advice given. According to many of the respondents, Dave Andrews needs to follow the university and/or departmental rules in dealing with extension requests, the case of suspected plagiarism and in deciding what to do about the gift. This would help to ensure consistency in the treatment meted out to students. In ensuring justice or *fairness*, and in modelling this virtue, he also needs to gather evidence and be quite sure of his facts before forming any hasty judgements about the incidents. In other words, Dave has a duty to facilitate what is sometimes termed 'natural justice': to hear all sides in investigating the various problems he faces. In some instances, such as the suspected plagiarism, this may also mean involving other academic staff as investigators not directly involved in making allegations of student cheating. Some process of investigation was regarded as of vital importance in handling the so-called 'free-rider' in the group or before making a judgement about the student he suspects of plagiarism.

While fairness or justice was perceived to be promoted by consistency in applying rules and procedures, at the same time, respondents highlighted the need for Dave to demonstrate *sensitivity* to the circumstances affecting individual students. Examples included showing an understanding of the pressures and probable family commitments of the mature student seeking an extension and in responding sympathetically to the case of the student with dyslexia who has asked for an extension. Sensitivity and understanding would also be needed in paying regard to cultural differences. These may explain different norms of behaviour among students with respect to the plagiarism and gift-giving incidents. The need for Dave to demonstrate an understanding of these cultural differences echoes the importance of *sensitivity* in the context of a tutorial relationship also identified in Chapter 4. Fundamentally, though, it was seen as vital to the credibility and authority of the lecturer for him to remain objective and be publicly seen to do so. Here, acceptance of the gift was perceived as potentially compromising this objectivity.

Finally, being fair was also defined in terms of justice to the majority of students, essentially mirroring a utilitarian rule of thumb. Requests for assignment extensions from individuals needed to be balanced against the unfairness this might represent to other students who had made strenuous efforts and proper provision of time to complete their work by the due date. Fairness to the majority was also a motivating factor behind several of the suggested solutions to the group dispute. The analysis of respondents indicates that fairness is a complex virtue to put into practice and demands a difficult balance to be maintained in managing the interests of students, both as individuals and as members of a larger group.

Chapter 6

Evaluating

Introduction

Trying to get students to think critically about subject knowledge or the nature of professional practice is central to the role of a teacher in higher education. It is an objective that many lecturers espouse (Nixon, 1996; Kolitch and Dean, 1999). However, until comparatively recently this notion of criticality has rarely been systematically and rigorously applied to teaching practice in university education. Committed individuals have always cared deeply about their own teaching and sought to continuously improve it, despite the absence of reward and recognition structures for doing so. Now though, there is a growing acceptance of the need to apply the academic principle of rigorous introspection to teaching as well as research. In the UK, over 12,000 higher education teachers are members of the ILTHE and are committed to the principle of 'reflective practice'. This implies continuously evaluating and, in the process, refining their teaching methods. Elsewhere, members of the Society for Teaching and Learning in Higher Education in Canada and the American Association of University Professors ascribe to similar values emphasizing the importance of maintaining and enhancing pedagogical competence. In short, evaluation of teaching is now recognized as a professional responsibility by higher education practitioners in many parts of the world.

Academics have long been accustomed to the processes of peer review in the context of their own research where judgements are reached about the quality of funding proposals and papers for publication. However, the use of systematic peer review in teaching is a more recent phenomenon. Peer review and teaching observation schemes are part of the changing landscape of higher education. Peer review refers to broader aspects of academic practice such as evaluation of curriculum materials and student assessments as well as classroom observation (Keig, 2000). Teaching observation schemes tend to be more limited in their objectives and focus on classroom presentation, facilitation and interaction. Another key difference between teaching observation schemes is that while some are essentially about formative assessment and the development of staff with the help of peers as 'buddies', other systems are aimed clearly at making a judgement about the teaching 'quality' of lecturers. They are essentially aimed at determining an individual's 'competence' to teach. This latter objective is often tied in with internal probation and review procedures or external review requirements. Hence, there are very different forms and purposes of peer review. These range from a narrow, 'checklist' approach to teaching observation for summative assessment of competence through to a process of collaborative, critical enquiry, involving peers, designed for formative assessment and enhancement of practice (Barnett, 1992).

At best, peer review processes supported by educational development act as an effective means of helping to critique aspects of practice in a supportive environment. A common pitfall, however, in the absence of support mechanisms, is to replicate and embed teaching practice which fails to progress the learning of students. Where teaching observation is used as the dominant method, a particular danger is the emphasis it gives to the 'performance' aspect of teaching rather than how effectively students are being helped to learn. Lecturer performance and student performance are not necessarily synonymous. However, when used in isolation, teaching observation can reinforce the false assumption that the two are identical.

Evaluation dilemmas

It has been argued that teaching in higher education is, essentially, a craft-based occupation rather than a profession since most attention is focused on inducting new members of the academic system into the existing system rather than involving all staff in a critical dialogue about teaching and learning methods (Elton, 2001). The use of peers to evaluate the teaching performance of colleagues in this context runs the risk of embedding orthodox assumptions about what constitutes 'good' teaching. Experienced professionals are not necessarily informed by a critical or intellectual understanding of teaching and learning theory. What they are informed by is current practice which may simply reinforce pedagogic tradition.

While teaching observation is the dominant method by which the performance of lecturers is evaluated, Student Evaluation Questionnaires (SEQs) are the principal means by which information about the quality of teaching is gathered from students (Clouder, 1998). It is a relatively low-cost method of providing information to stakeholders, such as students, parents, employers and government agencies (Wilson, Lizzio and Ramsden, 1997). Many writers, though, have warned against total reliance on the SEQ as the only tool for evaluating the quality of teaching (eg Centra, 1993). Ideally, a variety of methods should be deployed for evaluating and reflecting on the quality of teaching, not solely the SEQ (Timpson and Andrew, 1997).

Some researchers condemn the use of SEQs as a management tool that undermines rather than promotes professionalism. Johnson (2000) argues that where SEQs are imposed, managed and evaluated centrally, this dispossesses lecturers of control over their own practice and represents an affront to professional integrity:

> It (ie the SEQ) generates fear, damaged relationships and self-doubt, and is based on and appears to generate technicist concepts of teaching. It may have little additional impact in terms of a lecturer's professional development. Moreover, it promotes a concept of professional development as remedial action instigated by managers. It undermines and devalues a professional's own responsibility for initiating creative means of investigation that bear the authority of an individual professional's integrity and sense of relevance, and that generate action authorized on the basis of genuine interest, experiment and informed negotiation between the 'expert', their peers and their students.
>
> (Johnson, 2000: 433)

Another criticism of SEQs is that students are often the most conservative judges of teaching (Elton, 2001). Indeed, evidence indicates that introducing teaching methods, such as problem-based learning, which make greater demands on students in terms of goal setting and workload can result, to some extent, in poorer evaluation 'ratings' (Lyon and Hendry, 2002). SEQs are also considered to encourage a transmission model of education rather than one based on a critical pedagogy. Arguably, a 'good' lecture is one that probes and questions propositional or professional knowledge. This approach to lecturing challenges students to re-examine their own knowledge base rather than simply transferring information uncritically from the lecturer to the student. However, making learning challenging in this way may result in students feeling less, rather than more confident and positive about 'what they have learnt' from the lecture. This example serves to demonstrate that SEQs are not a value-neutral, 'scientific' way of collecting data about 'good' teaching (Kolitch and Dean, 1999).

A key criticism of relying too heavily on 'student-as-customer' perceptions in higher education is that learners are not always best placed to make evaluations in areas where they have no expert knowledge on which to base those judgements (Piercy, Lane and Peters, 1997). The literature on service management points out that there are some services that customers find difficult to evaluate, even after they have experienced the service (Lovelock, Vandermerwe and Lewis, 1996). For example, it is difficult for someone without knowledge of mechanics to assess whether they have had their car serviced satisfactorily immediately after this service has been performed. Only time will tell whether this service has been performed adequately, or if the vehicle splutters to a halt shortly afterwards. Higher education is a more complex professional service that is similarly difficult for the 'customer' to evaluate following 'consumption'. How, in other words, can students immediately judge the quality of their educational experience? Few will graduate having experienced higher education at another institution as a point of comparison. Graduates are normally only able to evaluate their experiences in a more informed manner some years after graduation when they have had an opportunity to reflect on the extent to which they have benefited, materially and emotionally, from the knowledge, skills and attitudes they developed while at university. This is often demonstrated in studies which ask alumni to assess their university or course experience (eg Coates and Koerner, 1996). Moreover, mature postgraduates are in a better position to compare the quality of their teaching at university based on their previous experiences of higher education.

Another ethical issue is the notion of 'game playing' whereby instructors concede benefits to students to get higher scores in evaluation (Piercy, Lane and Peters, 1997). Here, in a worst-case scenario, a kind of 'unholy alliance' can exist between students and the lecturer that, in return for giving learners an 'easy ride', they will support the teacher in evaluation and make fewer demands on his or her time. A perhaps less obvious form of game playing can occur both deliberately and inadvertently. Here, popular lecturers can benefit from the personal rapport they have with a group of students by being given more positive evaluation ratings than perhaps their teaching deserves. This so-called 'halo effect' can also operate in the opposite direction, with less popular but none the less effective teachers receiving poorer evaluation results than their performance merits (Orsini, 1988). At a deeper conceptual level, relying on students as principally responsible for evaluating teaching in higher education can undermine trust between students and teachers. In a trusting learning environment, the teacher, as well as the student, is open about his or her own sense of 'incompleteness, mistakes and confusion' (Curzon-Hobson, 2002: 275). Creating and sustaining this kind of environment, and teachers prepared to commit to this model of mutual learning, can be put under threat by placing the power of evaluation entirely in student hands.

Thus, while student evaluation of teaching is now widely accepted as *part* of good practice, there are dangers in being over-reliant on just one source of data. Here, therefore, it is important for university lecturers to apply their own knowledge of sound research principles. In getting at the truth, the triangulation of evidence – including peer review, student evaluation and teaching portfolios, as evidence of self-reflection and professional development – is no less important in teaching than it is in research.

A time to reflect?

Professor Stephanie Rae entered her room and let her stack of papers and books hit the desk with a satisfying thud. Reclining in her chair, she felt an overwhelming sense of relief. She had finally seen the back of the postgraduate research methods course for the term and could now get back to her 'real' work, as she saw it, by concentrating on a major new research grant proposal. The students had not been an easy group this year.

Stephanie had been appointed as a professor in Health Sciences at The University of Broadlands four years ago, having established an international reputation for her research work on evidence-based health care. Her busy professional life left her little time for other things, although Stephanie had always been a committed member of the Church of England. The research methods course was her only formal teaching commitment in addition to master's and doctoral supervision. Much of the rest of her time was spent working on various research projects, speaking at conferences, writing for publication and editing a major journal in her specialist field. However, although she had just finished teaching the research methods course, there was the little matter of the student evaluation questionnaires to consider. Sitting at her desk, Stephanie started to skim casually through the questionnaires which she had collected from the students at the end of the last session of her course. Departmental and university procedures required staff to evaluate their teaching and Stephanie's department used a standard questionnaire for all postgraduate courses. Lecturers (and professors!) are expected to collect this information, analyse the results and include this in their annual course report. While she could give these evaluations to one of the department's administrators to analyse, she usually felt a little embarrassed about letting someone else see them.

Reading the comments of her students, Stephanie became increasingly concerned. There were positives but quite a few complaints about 'boring readings' which were 'too theoretical'. There were also unfavourable comparisons made between Stephanie's approach and the way another, more junior colleague made lecture notes available on the Web and provided handouts of lecture slides in advance. Stephanie, though, had qualms about 'spoon feeding' the students in this way. There were also irritatingly low 'scores' from a minority of students who claimed not to understand the assessment process even though she had explained at length the role of this process in the course handbook. They were probably, Stephanie guessed, poor attenders who had got a low mark in their first assignment, a project proposal. Finally, following a teaching observation carried out by a colleague the previous term, she had tried to be 'innovative', with the encouragement of the university's Educational Development Unit, by getting the students to assess each other during oral presentations of research project outlines. However, several of the students complained that they were fed up with being used as 'guinea pigs' or being 'experimented on'. One student commented that 'Lecturers are paid to assess our work. Why on earth should we do it!' Momentarily, Stephanie felt tempted to dump some of the more unfair evaluations in the bin but wondered, resisting the urge, what she ought to do about the critical comments. She certainly did not have the time to spend ages rewriting the course with her research workload.

Recalling the last departmental committee meeting, she knew that 'quality' procedures had recently been overhauled and she was obliged to show in her 'action plan' how she would respond to these comments.

Stephanie wondered whether she should cave in, make things easier for the students and 'spoon feed' them more with notes and handouts and 'lighten up' the assessment demands. She certainly knew that this was the strategy recommended by one of her more cynical colleagues who was concerned about students taking his specialist option in sufficient numbers. As he had said to Stephanie, somewhat sarcastically, 'It's a popularity contest these days, Steph. It's about entertainment value and meeting "customer" expectations. Just give them what they want. They won't thank you for working them too hard.' Stephanie had agreed that students seemed to expect everything to be put on a plate for them now rather than doing hard research as she had been expected to do in completing her degrees.

Stephanie Rae faces a number of challenges in evaluating and changing her own teaching. As a mainly research-based academic she is, on the one hand, used to having the quality of her scholarly work reviewed by peers through activities such as submitting papers to journals for publication, writing books and applying for research funding. On the other hand, she is comparatively less accustomed to having the quality of her teaching challenged by students. Although, as a professor in a UK university (equivalent to a full professor in the United States), Stephanie is a senior academic, this status does not necessarily mean she possesses considerable teaching experience in higher education. She may be relatively inexperienced as a lecturer, with considerably more expertise as a clinical researcher. Stephanie's reaction to criticism from her students appears to be quite defensive. Evaluating practice implies a preparedness to accept criticism and to experiment with change. However, it is also important to note that what students consider important as a measure of teaching quality does not necessarily equate with the perceptions of university teachers (Ledic, Rafajac and Kovac, 1999). As with any other 'customer satisfaction' measurement, staff can feel alienated and threatened by the results of questionnaires, leading to the adoption of a dismissive attitude to criticism, the reinforcement of poor performance and game playing. Staff can perceive the process as allowing students to make a personal 'gripe' against the lecturer (Piercy, Lane and Peters, 1997). Stephanie Rae finds the criticism levelled against her teaching personally wounding. She is smarting from the comments of her students and appears inclined to react in a defensive way, blaming them for a lack of commitment or cynical motives. Here, there appears to be a great danger that Stephanie will not use the feedback from her students in a constructive way to improve her practice.

All respondents argued, to a greater or lesser extent, that Stephanie had an obligation to take the student evaluation of her teaching seriously. This was variously described as a 'professional responsibility' or about her 'honesty' or 'personal integrity'. While she may find some of the criticism harsh or personally hurtful, as a professional she should have an open mindset and be willing and interested in improving her practice. Moreover, she should not take the evaluation comments as a personal affront. A number of respondents suggested that she would benefit from discussing the student evaluations of her teaching quite openly with a (less cynical) colleague, with the student group as a whole or even with an external examiner or with a larger group of colleagues at a course or programme meeting. Stephanie clearly needs support from her colleagues in helping her to reflect on her practice.

Lecturers noted that part of the student criticism of her teaching related to her attempt to introduce student peer assessment. Here, the negative student comments indicated a lack of understanding of the purpose of the assessment in terms of their own learning. It was suggested that Stephanie ought to spend more time, in future, explaining the principles that lie behind the peer-assessed presentation in terms of the development of student skills and collective responsibility for teaching and learning. Trying out something new with students does involve elements of risk. Respondents argued, though, that Stephanie should not simply abandon innovation at the first hint of difficulty. Instead, she ought to look at explaining the principles better or modifying her approach in some way. Question marks were raised, however, about the extent to which Stephanie was really committed to the principles underpinning the use of peer assessment. If this is not the case then it is less likely that she could successfully convince her students of the value of this approach.

It was also stressed by many respondents that in reflecting on her practice Stephanie should not necessarily accept, in a 'supine' way, all of the criticism. For example, several respondents felt that making lecture notes available on the Web did not necessarily improve the quality of student learning. This might discourage rather than encourage students to engage actively in their own learning. In this respect they would encourage Stephanie to 'stick to her guns'. Instead of relying entirely on student evaluation as a basis for reflection and change, she should draw on other forms of evaluation, such as observation of her teaching (which is departmental policy), the comments of the external examiner and personal reflection.

Several respondents urged Stephanie to review her fundamental purpose as a university lecturer. These lecturers were concerned that Stephanie appeared to have a very traditional view of herself as a teacher. Given that one of her major concerns was not to 'spoon feed' her students, several lecturers suggested she ought to consider a more radical overhaul of her teaching and recommended enquiry-based or discovery methods as worth consideration. It is also important, in this context, for Stephanie's teaching innovations (in this case, peer assessment) to be aligned with her beliefs. She may, it was pointed out, have been coaxed into adopting peer assessment against her own instincts. Other respondents suggested that she should bring her own research into her teaching more. They argued that by doing this she would be more likely to inspire her students by illustrating her own commitment. This would counter student criticism about 'boring readings' and demonstrate her own passion for her subject.

Finally, while the majority of respondents saw nothing amiss with Stephanie personally administering and reviewing the questionnaire responses of her students, a significant number were critical of this approach. In their view, the process of distributing and collecting student feedback forms ought to be handled either by administrators within the department or institution or by student representatives. The analysis of the results of the questionnaire would then be carried out centrally and the results fed back to Stephanie. The advantage of such a system, it was pointed out, is that the temptation (which Stephanie feels) to tamper with the data is removed and the results can then be looked at in the overall context. For example, while Stephanie may think that her teaching compares unfavourably with that of other lecturers, the reality may be quite different from her perception. Adopting a more systematic approach may also mean that institution-wide issues causing students displeasure can be dealt with more effectively. It was clear from the divergent views of respondents on this issue that policy and practice in the administration of student evaluation vary widely across the UK higher education sector. While staff at some institutions are accustomed to a centralized system of student evaluation, elsewhere lecturers are administering and analysing feedback data themselves.

Most respondents, though, either did not comment about the need for the evaluation forms to be considered at departmental/institutional level or expressed reservations about the extent to which institution-wide systems are helpful in developing professional practice. The involvement of central or departmental processes in evaluation can be perceived as an invasive and bureaucratic intervention in the relationship between teachers and students, damaging trust and openness.

The charismatic lecturer

Stephanie was still wondering how she ought to respond to this set of critical evaluations as she made her way over to observe a lecture, by pre-arrangement with a colleague, as part of the department's 'quality enhancement' procedures. This required, among other things, reciprocal observations with a different colleague each academic year. Stephanie had certainly found it an eye-opener and had learnt a lot, she felt, in the process. The lecture turned out to be highly engaging and accomplished in many respects. It was well prepared and the students responded enthusiastically. They clearly found the lecturer, Max Schaefer, quite a charismatic speaker and, in fact, she knew that his course was extremely popular as he regularly got 'rave reviews' from students. However, Stephanie had qualms about its highly political nature. Max was overtly critical of a number of researchers and 'rubbished', she felt, the government's health-care research agenda. While he made a number of valid points, she was worried about over-generalizations which the students were apparently lapping up. When it came to questions from students towards the end, none of these sought to challenge the highly contentious nature of his lecture. She wondered, perhaps somewhat uncharitably, how well students would be treated if they wrote an essay or other assignment that took issue with his line of argument. While Stephanie needed to give Max some feedback following the observation, she knew, from previous contact with him, that he did not take kindly to criticism and that he was a firm believer in 'letting students know where I am coming from'. Looking at the teaching observation form she needed to fill in about 'pace of delivery', 'use of audiovisual equipment', etc, there was certainly no need to raise the issue on paper.

Max and Stephanie are two very different types of university lecturer. While Stephanie does not appear to integrate her research work into her teaching, Max is committed to a lecturing style that demonstrates his passion and ideological stance. As explained at the beginning of the chapter, one of the key ways in which university teachers define their role is in terms of getting students to think critically about knowledge. However, as illustrated by Stephanie and Max, there are very different ways of achieving this. Stephanie, through what we know about her own teaching and her concerns about Max, appears to favour an approach based on what is sometimes referred to as 'neutrality' or being 'balanced' (Hanson, 1996). She does not think it is right for teachers to preach their own political views to students. Stephanie appears to have a genuine concern that the academic freedom of the students, to express alternative perspectives, may be adversely affected by Max's teaching style. This, in turn, may lead to students thinking there is only one 'right' answer that coincides with Max's views.

On the other hand, Max is clearly considered an inspirational teacher by his students. One of the likely reasons for this is that he is demonstrating his passion for his subject. Evidence suggests that students respond well to lecturers who are able to convey their enthusiasm for their subject. In response to any criticism from Stephanie, it is possible that Max may argue that it would be intellectually dishonest if he sought to hide his personal views. He is, after all, being open about his ideological stance rather than trying to pretend that he does not have one, a criticism which he might well level against lecturers who seek to hide their commitments or values if challenged on the issue.

This vignette provoked considerable debate among respondents who recognized the delicate nature of the problem that Stephanie faces. Almost all suggested that the matter would best be handled through an informal, debriefing discussion rather than through use of the observation form. Words like 'tact', 'diplomacy' and 'sensitivity' were used to express the personal qualities Stephanie would need in handling this situation effectively and professionally. It was also suggested that one way of building an understanding and respect between Max and Stephanie might be through observation of each other's teaching. This would build a better understanding between them and allow for both teachers to learn in the process. The responses stressed the importance of dealing with the difference of approach (or opinion) in handling personal convictions outside the 'public' nature of the teaching observation form in a personal, sensitive and collegial manner. Ironically, however, it was noted that while Max does 'not take kindly to criticism', neither, it appears, does Stephanie on the basis of her own reaction to student feedback.

There are significant emotions being played out here as part of this vignette. Stephanie, it was suggested, may well be jealous of Max's cult status and the fact that he is getting 'rave reviews' from the students. She may also sense that Max is benefiting from the 'halo effect' in his student evaluations while she is refusing to give her students an 'easy ride'. Max may also, it was argued, be reacting emotionally to the presence of Stephanie in his lecture room, which he may resent or feel uncomfortable about for various reasons of his own. As a result, his behaviour on this occasion may even be quite untypical of his normal lecturing style.

In handling the situation, some respondents argued that Stephanie should not jump to too many conclusions. For example, Max's lecturing style may contrast sharply with his approach in facilitating a smaller group discussion. Here, he might encourage alternative opinions to be aired and his own position to be subject to critical interrogation. Other aspects to the course Max teaches may indicate greater balance and openness to debate, such as the reading list or the assessment task(s) set. This point demonstrates the inadequacy of relying on a 'snapshot', such as a teaching observation, to gain a proper insight into the complex reality of a course.

Most respondents articulated a 'middle way' between Stephanie's concerns about any form of politicization and Max's open advocacy of one particular standpoint. They argued that while it is important to be honest with students about one's own ideological or political position, it should be made clear that this is only one of several possible positions on an issue and that critical engagement with all positions is actively encouraged. This position is illustrated in the comments of three of my respondents, shown in Figure 6.1.

In this situation, the importance of the lecturer acting as a role model for students (Ottewill, 2001) is vitally important. One way of demonstrating the type of critical engagement expected of students is for the lecturer to show the weaknesses of a position that the teacher himself holds dear (Hanson, 1996). Being the 'devil's advocate' in this way demonstrates to students that no view is sacrosanct or beyond the bounds of a reasoned argument. The position articulated by

Individuals should be encouraged to adopt an innovative and lively lecturing style, but it is dangerous to adopt a style (and content) which means the students are not encouraged to see all sides of an argument and make up their own minds about particular issues and debates.

While taking a particular line is acceptable if the goal is to stimulate reactions from students, it should always be made clear to them (ie the students) that it is a personal stance and that they are free to challenge it in discussions and assessed work. In these circumstances there is always the danger that students will be overawed and that instead of being empowered the expert–novice relationship will be reinforced.

While you can agree that students can know where you are coming from, surely it is unprofessional not to present both sides of the argument to stimulate the argument – isn't that what higher education is about?

Figure 6.1

respondents was broadly similar to that advocated by Brookfield (1987) that the ideological position of the teacher should not get in the way of helping students to interrogate values and beliefs which may previously have been considered not open to challenge.

As an academic, Stephanie has a clear self-image. She is a researcher first and foremost and teaching plays, at best, a minor part in her daily life. She has religious convictions but these beliefs do not noticeably appear to shape her approach to teaching. Some respondents commented that Stephanie appeared to be something of a loner or a 'solitary character'. This has obvious disadvantages in view of the feedback she received from her students and the benefits to be derived from supportive colleagues who can help her reflect on her practice. Her critical view of Max's passionate advocacy suggests someone who believes that personal beliefs should not play a major role in teaching.

Conclusion

Reflective practice has become a modern mantra used to express the responsibility of professionals, including teachers in higher education, to adopt an open attitude and invest effort in the improvement of practice. However, meeting this requirement represents a considerable challenge to many lecturers accustomed to a more traditional expert–novice relationship with students rather than one based on an open learning partnership. In interpreting the requirement to 'reflect', respondents warned against extreme emotional reactions: defensive, intellectual disengagement through a failure to listen to criticism at one extreme and an over-reactive response to all critical feedback resulting in the abandonment of innovation or key principles at the other. Neither of these positions is genuinely reflective. Instead, respondents recommended *openness* to criticism and new ideas, while not losing sight of a commitment to legitimately different personal teaching philosophies. It is important to listen and act where appropriate but not to succumb unreflectively or supinely. The customer, in other words, is not always right.

The other main issue raised in this chapter relates to a passion for ideas. Wanting to communicate a passion for a subject is a laudable goal. Indeed, it is a goal that attracts many to an academic career. Lecturers who fail to communicate their passion or commitment to their subject are unlikely to inspire their students. But, as Nelson and Watt (1999) point out, good teaching is about the successful combination of passion and reason or 'passionate reason'. Too much 'passion' for an ideological position may stifle the development of student critical reasoning. Part of this case study has illustrated the importance of getting that balance right. Thus, lecturers should guard against being 'shrinking violets' about their ideological stance on the one hand and becoming inadvertent 'intellectual bullies' on the other. Rather, the position suggested by respondents is one of *restraint*. This means being honest about one's own intellectual or ideological position while reassuring students and modelling critical engagement with *all* positions. Only a learning environment free from the perception or reality of intellectual prejudice will enable students to develop their own critical voice. Naturally, this extends beyond the classroom and must also be a living commitment of all institutions of higher education and societies in which they operate. Without adequate safety and reassurance self-censorship may occur among staff as well as students (Cheng, 1995).

Finally, responses to the case study reveal some significant differences in individual attitudes and institutional cultures. Again, as in previous case studies, there was a marked contrast between individuals accustomed to working in an institutional environment with a greater emphasis on standardized rules and procedures and those where practice is more informal. In particular, this was illustrated by the fact that some respondents were clearly familiar with a system of more centralized evaluation where the lecturer is removed from the collection and analysis of feedback data. While such centralization can help to systematize evaluation processes and allow for more meaningful comparison of data, it can also represent an obstacle to innovation and undermine the trust necessary for a genuinely open and rigorous dialogue between students and teachers.

Chapter 7

Managing

Introduction

The word 'management' has negative connotations for many academics working in higher education. It represents a shift away from the ancient ideal of university life as a free-associating collective of individuals and towards a centralization of executive power based on market principles (Halsey, 1992). Academic management, traditionally characterized in terms of consensus and collegiality and the sharing of decision making, has given way to 'new managerialism' (Dearlove, 1995). Managerial power has increasingly replaced the traditional autonomy of academics to govern their own affairs. University vice-chancellors are now routinely compared with corporate chief executives. Some even adopt the title. While the word 'administration' denotes a benign and neutral exercise of authority, the term 'management' is associated, by many in academia, with more directive and less consensual decision-making processes paying closer attention to market forces. Nevertheless, the term represents a very real change in the relationship of universities to the societies they serve. Increasingly, universities must compete as educational providers in an environment in which national governments regard higher education institutions as instruments of their exacting social and economic policy. The communications revolution means that universities now compete more internationally for students and research income both with each other and with a growing number of corporate education and independent training providers. However, the notion of universities as self-regulating communities still has strong roots which continue to exert a powerful influence within certain institutions, such as the Universities of Oxford and Cambridge, where controversies regarding the reform of governance structures have raged in recent years.

At the level of the university department or school, academic staff have long exercised 'administrative' or 'managerial' roles as Deans, Heads of Department, committee Chairs, admissions tutors, course directors and so on. As the demands of modern university life have changed owing to increasing competition and external accountability, so new management roles have emerged at departmental or faculty level such as that of the marketing manager, quality assurance officer and director of teaching and learning. However, academics are primarily a community of scholars who come together voluntarily to study and learn (Barnett, 1992). Few enter the profession to pursue a managerial career. Power and respect in academic life have traditionally derived from scholarly expertise rather than managerial responsibilities. This, combined with principles of collegiality, with its emphasis on shared decision making, is why many of these roles have traditionally been rotated between staff. It also means that being required to perform a managerial role can be regarded as an unwelcome distraction, rather than a reward or accolade, since such responsibilities are in contrast with the motivating factors that brought individuals into academia in the first place, such as a desire to teach or research. However, managing, for all its negative associations, is now an inescapable component of modern academic practice (Blaxter, Hughes and Tight, 1998). It is as much a feature of modern academic life as teaching or research.

Course management dilemmas

This chapter will focus on the ethical challenges associated with managing a course or programme of study rather than the management of institutions at a senior level. This involves management of both students and academic colleagues. The nature of collegiality means that the positional authority of many of those charged with management functions at departmental level is frequently greater than their scholarly status. This means that they are asked to manage more senior academic colleagues and, as the case study demonstrates, gives rise to particular challenges for those placed in such a position.

A safe pair of hands

Dr Dilip Patel has worked at The University of Broadlands as a Senior Lecturer in Mechanical Engineering for six years. He had started his lecturing job at the university after spending three years working for the research and development department of a major corporation following graduation and a period as a volunteer for an international aid organization. The time since seems to have flown by, although the papers Dilip had planned to publish, based on his doctoral work on biofluidmechanics, are still languishing, half-written, on his hard drive. He had felt pretty swamped at first getting to grips with the demands of being a lecturer and taking responsibility for 'quality assurance' just prior to the inspection of the department last year. He had been surprised when, just before the beginning of term, he had been made the programme director of one of the department's major undergraduate degrees. The Head of Department had said that he was pleased by his progress and wanted to show his confidence in Dilip as a 'safe pair of hands' by giving him senior responsibility. When he had raised his concern about workload and his desire to become more research 'active', the Head had said it was important for him to 'pitch in' on administrative duties and gain experience as a programme director. Besides which, now that the inspection was over, he would be asking someone else in the department to take on the quality role.

Things seemed to be going satisfactorily so far in his new role. There had been a number of niggling problems with timetable clashes and complaints about rooming arrangements from students (too small, too hot, etc) but that, colleagues assured him, was quite normal. Today, though, had been a difficult one.

It all started in the most unexpected way with a knock at his office door. He had been pleased to see Claire Stevens, a bright and conscientious final-year student, who had rung to book the appointment with him a few days before. Relaxed, he leant back in his chair. He was not expecting the bombshell to come. Claire explained that she had come to see him about the marks received by the whole class for a particular module. This third-year module was one taught by Professor Bland, an experienced senior member of staff who had worked in the department for over 20 years. The module was a final-year option for which Dilip had overall responsibility as programme director. Claire explained that she was there on behalf of the whole class even though she had not received a low mark herself. She had got 60 per cent. This took Dilip aback. He had become accustomed to individual students coming along on the odd occasion to complain about a low mark they had received for this or that assignment but he had never encountered this situation. Claire went on to explain that hardly anyone in the group had received a mark above 40 per cent for that module's assignment and most students had got a mark of between 30 and 40 per cent. Many of the students, she said, who were accustomed to receiving average marks in the 50s and 60s, were concerned that this low mark would affect their degree result and could mean that several would fall below the class of degree they needed to secure conditional job and postgraduate study offers. When Dilip asked whether she or anyone else from the group had spoken with the module tutor, she replied that they had tried but had been rebuffed in a dismissive way. Dilip knew that the assignments had been second marked already and wondered what, if anything, he ought to do about the situation. Claire had not come to see him on her own behalf but for the benefit of others in the group but there were clearly delicate issues here. Dilip recalled that he had recently overheard part of an exchange between Professor Bland and a student while passing his office. He had heard Professor Bland saying, in a sarcastic and rhetorical way, 'I suggest you start by doing some reading. After all, if I am not mistaken, you're meant to be reading for a degree. Or don't students read these days?' Looking at his watch, Dilip realized that there were only five minutes to go before he was due to chair the Staff–Student Liaison Committee and, assuring Claire that he would get back to her, ended the meeting. Quite what he could do about this situation, though, was another matter.

Like many academics managing courses in higher education, Dilip would probably rather be spending this time away from teaching and working on his research. He has also not received any professional development to carry out the role of a course manager. While many courses in educational development focus on the teaching role, few pay much attention to wider aspects of 'academic practice' connected with teaching, such as course management. He is also a comparatively junior member of staff who probably does not yet feel sufficiently confident to decline the role offered to him as little more than a *fait accompli* by his Head of Department. This is symptomatic of what Hargeaves (1994) has termed 'contrived' collegiality where decisions are based on power relations rather than genuinely collaborative decision-making processes. The result is that Dilip has been told to take on a role that is not of his choosing.

One of the main problems Dilip faces is how to exercise the considerable responsibilities of this new role with what appears to be limited power and authority. He is, as the case study starts to demonstrate, responsible for managing a course team of academics of varying levels of seniority. He is not a senior member of the department but needs to be able to manage his colleagues effectively while maintaining their respect and cooperation.

While most respondents made it clear that they had concerns about how Dilip had been allocated his new duties by his Head of Department, most argued that course management was part of the reality of being a modern academic. This was defined by some as part of the third 'service' element of an academic's role, with the other two being teaching and research respectively. However, most respondents argued that Dilip should not tamely accept his new professional responsibilities without entering into a proper negotiation with the Head of Department to ensure that he receives adequate remission from other duties as a *quid pro quo*. He also needs to clarify the scope of his authority to carry out the role adequately. Most respondents suggested that he needed a more explicit and less one-sided deal with his Head of Department to cope with the role. It was recognized that academic course managers can frequently be placed in an almost impossible position by being given 'responsibility without authority'. Others contended that Dilip should ensure that the Head of Department understands that research remains a key personal priority for him, with a small minority suggesting that he should refuse to perform the course management role altogether or start looking for a new job outside the institution given the circumstances.

Turning to the specific issues raised in this vignette, Dilip faces an immediate and very real problem in seeking to resolve the concern about the grading of assignments brought to him by Claire. As Kennedy has commented, 'no single issue raises more hostility in the teacher–student relationship than the management of grading disputes' (1997: 82). He offers his own advice as to how to deal with such situations:

The first is to be compassionate even when it is necessary to be firm. A second is to preserve the rights of everyone while dealing with the individual complaint. (For example, there are serious problems in agreeing to regrade one essay in a small class without reevaluating the others.) A third is always to admit the possibility of error, and to permit the student a fair opportunity to show that there has been one. A fourth is not to be arbitrary. The deepest resentments that develop over grading disputes result from situations in which a frustrated or worn-out professor has delivered the equivalent of the Parent's retort: 'Why? Because I said so, damn it!'. And most important, if there is a policy, it should be advertised up front, so everyone knows what it is. (1997: 83)

Clearly, as Kennedy points out, it is vital to keep in mind key principles such as fairness to all students and consistency in dealing with relevantly similar matters. Respondents emphasized the importance of several of the points made by Kennedy, particularly the need to investigate the facts before making any accusations or rushing to an early judgement and either re-evaluating (and potentially regrading) all assignments or none. Just one respondent suggested confronting Professor Bland about the grading of the assignments on the basis of Claire's claims without first assembling solid evidence of a genuine concern. In this sense, the advice of respondents echoes the emphasis on investigation to establish the true facts in relation to the cases of alleged 'free-riding' and suspected plagiarism considered in Chapter 5.

There was very variable advice, though, as to *how* Dilip should proceed. This advice included checking the marks for the course, seeing a larger group of students from the course, sending a sample of assignments to the external examiner, meeting directly with Professor Bland or sharing the problem with a colleague. A number of lecturers recommended a combination of these strategies. There were divergent views as to the role of the external examiner. While some respondents saw this person's role as legitimately arbitrating in such a circumstance, others made it explicit that they should not be involved. Some respondents also suggested seeking the help and advice of the Head of Department. However, there were concerns expressed that this could be interpreted as a 'cry for help' or as a 'sign of weakness' that Dilip was incapable of handling the issue. The concern of respondents here was that such a move could potentially undermine the Head's confidence in Dilip as a 'safe pair of hands' and adversely affect his future prospects for advancement.

Second or double marking of assignments is a traditional check on subjectivity in assessment practice. It is also a means of controlling lecturers who are proud of their reputation as a 'hard' marker (Partington, 1994). In some ways it is reassuring for Dilip that the student assignments have already been second marked. This offers a measure of protection against student appeals. Less positively, however, 'convergence' between two markers is more likely to occur when the second marker is privy to the grading and comments of the first marker (Partington, 1994). Moreover, Professor Bland's status as a senior academic adds a further layer of social pressure for convergence, assuming that the second marker is a more junior colleague. In the longer term, Dilip might consider the case for introducing 'blind' double marking, where the second marker works without pre-knowledge of the first marker's judgement and comments. This helps to guard against convergence. It was also suggested that an underlying cause of the current student dispute might be the absence of sufficiently explicit assessment criteria used when setting assignments within the course. Assessment criteria can serve as an effective and transparent means of explaining expectations, giving clearer student feedback and justifying grading decisions.

The issue confronting Dilip represented a dilemma of loyalties for many respondents. While it was seen as important that Dilip took his responsibilities to the students seriously and investigated Claire's allegation, it was felt that he was also under an obligation to demonstrate due respect to his (more senior) colleague, Professor Bland. Handling this issue in a sensitive and fair way to all parties was regarded as vital. As we will see in the next vignette, trying to manage more senior colleagues places Dilip in a particularly difficult situation.

The Staff–Student Committee meeting

Things went from bad to worse. The Staff–Student Committee did not go well. Despite explaining at the outset that the committee's role was to 'identify general issues and find practical solutions in a positive atmosphere', several of the student representatives had been quite scathing in their criticism of one of the teaching team, absent from the meeting. Although this member of staff was not mentioned by name, everyone present knew who was being talked about. The comments were clearly aimed at Dr Brunton, a part-time, visiting lecturer who had considerable expertise in his specialist field and was a busy, practising professional. He was also a close personal friend of the Head of Department. They had known each other since studying at the same university back in the early 1970s and working together on post-doctoral work. The students complained that the second-year module for which Dr Brunton was responsible was badly organized and that lectures were frequently cancelled without notice. When they had tried to raise these issues with 'the module leader' (ie Dr Brunton) they had been told to 'grow up and start living in the real world!' Dilip responded that he would investigate the students' concerns, although privately he doubted that he would get very far. He was only too well aware of Dr Brunton's friendship with the Head of Department and, anyway, it would be hard to replace someone with Dr Brunton's expertise on a part-time basis. He hoped his response would help to take the heat out of what was rapidly becoming an increasingly tense atmosphere. Unfortunately, one of the student representatives pressed, 'so you will talk to Dr Brunton then?' At this point, the former programme director intervened sharply, telling the student that 'this is not the forum for making personal comments'. This remark led to an unexpected outburst from the third-year representative who said angrily: 'This meeting is just the usual farce. It's the same, year after year. We complained about Brunton last year and nothing happened. All you lecturers ever do is close ranks when anyone makes any criticism of your teaching. What's the point of this meeting? What's the point?' He then promptly walked out of the room. This incident caused a great deal of embarrassment and the meeting came to a fairly rapid conclusion. Resolving this issue and restoring the students' confidence in the work of the committee would clearly be no easy matter.

Although such a fractious meeting is (hopefully!) not an everyday occurrence, the concerns of the students represent a very real issue which Dilip has a professional obligation to take seriously. There are a lot of accusations flying around about Dr Brunton and, as in the first vignette, careful and deliberate investigation was recommended by all respondents. It was agreed that although Dr Brunton has been portrayed as an uncaring and uncooperative individual by the students, it is important that Dilip does not jump to any hasty conclusions. On the other hand, doing nothing is also an unacceptable response. It is important that certain facts can be checked first. Is there evidence that lectures have been regularly cancelled? Are there Student Evaluation Questionnaires from this year or last which highlight similar problems? If the problems are real, do they feed through into poor results on Dr Brunton's module? These, and many other questions were raised by respondents as important in getting at the truth of the matter.

It was also stressed by several respondents that it is important to look at the root causes of the outburst at the meeting. At one level, this could be due to a lack of communication between staff and students where insufficient opportunities have arisen for concerns to be aired in the past. The incident begs the question as to whether there is an effective system of evaluation operating within the department that leads to real change in response to criticism. There may also be a lack of teamwork or a 'team ethos' operating within the department. Why has this issue got to such a stage without previously being identified as a problem and addressed by the teaching team? The criticism of Dr Brunton may also, it was pointed out, be indicative of a lack of development and induction processes for part-time or visiting lecturers. Has Dr Brunton, in other words, received adequate support to carry out his role properly as a part-time lecturer? Finally, the explanation for the cancelled lectures could be due to a lack of planning or adaptability and rectifiable by moving the lecture to a different day and/or time of the week when it would better suit Dr Brunton, with the cooperation of the students.

In terms of immediate advice, it was again stressed that Dilip should investigate the matter carefully both through meeting with the individual parties concerned and in checking the facts (eg whether lectures have been cancelled). Additionally, a 'clear the air' meeting between all parties, with the students and Dr Brunton present, was suggested by several individual respondents. Intervening with a colleague in this way runs risks similar to those faced by Stephanie Rae in the last chapter but represents a more acute situation for Dilip given Dr Brunton's status within the department. In acting, Dilip needs to adopt similar principles to those identified in relation to Dave Andrews' suspected plagiarism dilemma (Chapter 5). These include being sure of one's ground by marshalling the evidence, consulting with more experienced colleagues and giving Dr Brunton the opportunity to explain and defend how the situation has arisen. These are principles similar to those suggested by Keith-Spiegel *et al* (1996) in confronting colleagues.

Overall, the advice fell into two categories with regard to this incident. This consisted of working to resolve the immediate problem in the short term and, secondly, ensuring that this kind of situation did not reoccur in the future. In dealing with the short term, Dilip needs to take the student concerns seriously, investigate their complaints thoroughly and then act to resolve the issue at hand. In the longer term, and more fundamentally, suggestions included better communication between students and staff, encouraging a teamwork ethos among the lecturers contributing to the course and evaluating the development needs of staff, including part-time lecturers.

The innovative colleague

Back in his office, Dilip started to turn his mind to a different issue involving the teaching of a junior colleague on the degree programme for which he was responsible. This term, Dilip had been acting as a 'second marker' on Dr Greening's module and it had been something of a revelation. Dr Greening had been teaching at the university for the past 18 months and she had taken over a well-established module from a senior member of the department who had recently retired. Dr Greening had made substantial changes to the module, increasing the use of active learning techniques, group work and the use of technical reports in assessment to reflect the challenges of professional practice. These innovations had been popular with students. This year, substantially more students had chosen to undertake her module. As a result, some of the more traditionally organized modules, using lectures and laboratory work and assessed largely by individual assignments and examinations, had barely sufficient numbers of students to be economically viable. Also, the rate of innovation on Dr Greening's module was such that it no longer conformed to departmental rules and procedures. The examination had been scrapped and the assessment was completely by coursework. This consisted of a group technical report, a group oral presentation and a mark awarded to students on the basis of their 'contribution in class'. While Dilip wanted to encourage innovation, he did not want it to backfire and alienate colleagues in quite a traditional and conservative teaching environment. The loss of students to Dr Greening's module had already caused some resentment among other staff and moves were afoot within the department to bring the assessment of the module back into line with departmental procedures by raising the issue at the next departmental Board of Studies. Questions had been raised about how the external examiner could verify student achievement on the basis of oral presentations and 'class contribution' grades, among other criticisms. Dr Greening clearly had a lot to contribute to the development of the department's teaching but Dilip needed to ensure that the rate of innovation did not alienate the more traditionally minded members of staff. He needed to speak with Dr Greening and badly needed to think of a way forward to sort out this issue before matters came to a head.

Dr Greening is clearly an individual who has a lot to offer the course and Dilip's department as a whole. She possesses creativity and a flair for innovation. All managers need to find a way of utilizing the energy and creativity of people like Dr Greening. The balancing act which Dilip needs to perform here is to find a way of encouraging Dr Greening while ensuring that the changes which her innovations promise are both manageable and accepted by her colleagues. The essential virtue here, and indeed elsewhere in this case study, is collegiality. While her innovations are praiseworthy, in some respects there is a need for a degree of consensus in the department in decision making about assessment procedures. Many respondents were concerned that currently Dr Greening was out of step with agreed university and/or departmental procedures and needed to be 'reined in'.

Several respondents argued that Dilip should use the opportunity to encourage debate within the department about teaching and assessment methods. Dr Greening's popularity with the students indicates that colleagues could learn from her ideas. Suggestions for harnessing Dr Greening's talent and enthusiasm included asking her to present a paper at the next meeting of the course committee to demonstrate the practical benefits of her assessment methods. This would have the advantage of bringing her practice into the open and engaging colleagues in a debate about possible change which could be beneficial to both students and lecturers.

While Dr Greening's preparedness to experiment with her assessment methods was regarded as a positive or even courageous act, this should not be done at the expense of consistency and fairness to the students. The use of a 'contribution in class' grade was viewed as a potentially unfair form of assessment in this context. This criticism relates, probably at least in part, to the fact that most respondents were drawn from a UK higher education context, although such a means of contributing to the grading of students is in more widespread use in the United States.

The vignette highlights a subtext of jealousy and suspicion among colleagues. There is a suggestion that Dr Greening's course is gaining in popularity at the expense of others and this raises the danger that some will oppose her innovation for self-regarding rather than intellectual reasons. Overcoming the resentment that may be building against her was seen as a key challenge for Dilip. The longer-term strategy that Dilip should consider, according to some who commented on the case, is to foster a closer but more open teaching team ethos. Holding regular but relatively informal meetings for 'brainstorming' about new teaching and assessment ideas might help to build trust and communication between staff, leading to greater acceptance of innovation and ensuring that pedagogic decision making is collaborative rather than purely personal.

Conclusion

This case study highlights the problems of course management in a context of 'contrived' collegiality (Hargreaves, 1994). Dilip appears to have little choice but to take on this role even though he would rather be expending his energy on research. However, like Lesley Chung (see Chapter 4), Dilip's relatively junior status within the department and embryonic rather than established research record place him in a vulnerable position. Rightly or wrongly, course management is widely regarded as a tiresome task rather than a professional reward. There is clearly a problem of communication and this applies equally to relations between staff as to those between staff and the student body.

Dilip appears to be very isolated, or dissociated from the aid of his colleagues, and left with difficult decisions to make on his own. Almost all respondents strongly recommended the importance of Dilip seeking out the help, advice and support of his colleagues as critical to resolving any of these issues. Collective responsibility for the management of students is central to academic life and the concept of *collegiality*. Although principally defined by respondents in terms of relationships with colleagues, this term should not imply a cosy 'closing of ranks' by academic staff, a view clearly expressed by the students in the case study. A collegial disposition in terms of course management needs to engage others, both staff and students, in decision-making processes and avoid the vices of being either too dissociated from others or working as part of a cliquey cabal. Instead, collegiality needs to be redefined as joint decision making by all members of the academic community, including students.

Finally, the situation demands that Dilip needs to possess *courage* as a course manager to bring about change where justified and confront, where evidence demands it, more senior members of the teaching team. This is no easy task. Here, in referring to the importance of courage, a willingness to compromise and find an acceptable solution for all is perhaps as much a signal of this virtue as an obstinate refusal to broker any settlement (Solomon, 1992). It is only through gaining the trust and respect of colleagues, especially senior members of the department, that Dilip will ultimately succeed in this challenging task.

Part 3

Identifying the virtues

Chapter 8

Points of departure

Introduction

The preceding section of this book sought to illustrate and analyse some of the ethical dilemmas faced by university lecturers in their practice. The purpose of this chapter is to reflect on the different ways in which university lecturers seek to resolve the ethical issues that they confront as part of their professional practice. These will provide 'points of departure' in relation to the role of rules and discretion in decision making as well as contrasting perspectives on 'emotion' and 'distance' in teaching. It draws on the results of 'road testing' the case studies which appeared in the last section of this book, together with previous publications by the author (Macfarlane, 2001, 2002). These 'road tests', as noted earlier, have consisted of specially assembled focus groups, workshops at successive conferences of the UK Institute for Learning and Teaching in Higher Education, and academic development programmes at both City University, London and Canterbury Christ Church University College, together with responses from selected individuals. Thus, several hundred higher education teachers from a variety of different universities and subject areas have contributed to discussion of these cases. While they represent a sample based on opportunity and convenience rather than scientific principles, my respondents do comprise a good mix on the basis of levels of seniority, nationality, gender and disciplinary background.

In discussing the various case studies, clear differences emerged between lecturers in the way in which they perceive and respond to ethical dilemmas in their teaching, but there were also, perhaps more importantly, principles of agreement. This chapter will analyse different styles in resolving the ethical dilemmas of teaching on campus and particular points of departure between my respondents with respect to key issues. It will also seek to link this discussion to the broader context of change in higher education.

Proficiency and principles

The first reaction of some of my respondents to the various case studies was to question whether they really involved any 'ethical' issues. Were they not, these respondents suggested, more simply illustrative of the need to provide lecturers with professional development? In other words, Lesley, Dave, Stephanie and Dilip appeared to be relatively inexperienced individuals who faced problems connected with a lack of pedagogic knowledge and professional experience. It was argued that many of these problems could be resolved by using a variety of techniques. For example, a more active learning approach would provide a 'safer' environment to elicit responses from all members of the class in Chapter 4 and getting students to peer assess individual contributions to group work was recommended in relation to the group dispute in Chapter 5. However, while such techniques may help to minimize the chances of ill-considered remarks being made in open discussion and arguments developing between groups of students, they will never eliminate the possibility entirely. Indeed, some educators committed to experiential learning argue that deliberately creating a 'trauma', such as a dysfunctionally large student group to work on a task, positively promotes learning and personal growth (November, 1997).

Interpreting the case studies purely in terms of pedagogic process development is symptomatic of the way in which teaching is still viewed by many practitioners as a craft-based, technical skill rather than a fully rounded professional activity necessarily involving ethical choices and dilemmas. The vast majority of my respondents, though, did see the cases as about more than the provision of additional staff development to the various protagonists. Clearly the line between professional proficiency and ethical conscience is a thin one (Weber, 1995), although any rounded definition of professionalism must include both.

While many respondents recognized that the case studies raised issues beyond the realms of professional proficiency or competency, they also found it understandably difficult to articulate the ethical and/or professional principles which underpin the advice they offered to the fictitious case study characters. This, again, may be related to the fact that while university teachers deal with ethical problems on a daily basis, they do not belong to a tightly knit and well-defined profession that devotes formal attention to its ethical stance. Interestingly, when pressed to articulate the values that underpinned their advice, many respondents referred to ethical principles derived from a range of professional identities such as lawyers, psychologists and health practitioners. They were aware of codes of ethics and/or professional principles governing their behaviour in this other professional capacity but not in relation to university teaching.

Discretion and rules

One of the most notable differences to emerge in discussion of the cases was between teachers who tended primarily to emphasize the importance of following university procedures and policies with respect to the issues raised and those who advocated a more personal or individualized approach to problem solving using greater professional autonomy. While lecturers tended to identify the importance of similar basic character traits, such as sensitivity or fairness (see Chapter 9), they articulated different perspectives in relation to practising such virtues. The dichotomy between 'rules' and 'discretion' parallels the analysis provided by Stone and Wehlage (1982) in relation to dilemmas in schooling. They discuss the dualism of 'objective' and 'subjective' authority. Objective authority stems from the universal application of institutional rules whereas subjective authority refers to the more 'informal and particularistic' application of rules which takes account of extenuating or personal circumstances.

Many respondents commented on the need, as they saw it, for the case study characters to be aware of and follow the department and/or university rules. They were absolutist (Forsyth, 1980) in their attitude to decision making, having no truck with making exceptions on the basis of individual circumstances. These lecturers argued that the goal of being fair to students could only be achieved by strict adherence to such regulations. They were generally unwilling to make exceptions to university rules affecting staff and students. For example, in the case study about assessment issues, a number of lecturers argued that

deadlines should be strictly applied regardless of the personal circumstances of the student and that gifts should never be accepted. The
plagiarism issue was approached by some respondents as purely a
matter of following the prescribed course of action according to
university regulations. These respondents were far less sympathetic to
the personal circumstances affecting individual students but argued
that the goal of fairness could only be achieved through absolute
consistency. Many of the lecturers who advocated the importance of
universal rules to promote equality and fairness, such as assignment
deadlines or punishing plagiarism, were, though, prepared to admit
circumstances where they might make exceptions. These exceptions,
however, were also based on following the rules, such as being
prepared to extend an assignment deadline on the basis of certified
illness. Evidence, by definition, would need to be persuasive, such as
the production of a medical certificate. Underlying this position is a
belief that to make exceptions would be unfair on other students who
have abided by the rules. In a sense this is a utilitarian rationale that
the moral rule must be upheld in the interests of the majority, rule-
abiding students.

The importance of consistency and rule-abiding behaviour in arriving at decisions was reflected in other case study incidents. The same
respondents were often critical of Dr Greening, Dilip's 'innovative'
colleague in the case study concerned with course management, for
developing new approaches to assessment without recourse to the
standard rules governing such practices (see Chapter 7). Here, a
failure to consult other colleagues was also cited as a practice likely to
lead to inconsistent, and hence unfair, assessment practices. Three of
my respondents gave a clear rationale for their insistence on a rule-
bound approach to decision making:

> One of the advantages of working for a large organization is that you don't
> have to make major policy decisions yourself, and that, even where the
> decision-making process is cumbersome, there is some due process and
> some consideration given to what ramifications the decision would have.

> Lecturers, no matter how well intentioned they are, should adhere to the
> university's rules and regulations for assessment. This ensures consistency
> and fairness across courses and programmes.

> Don't take this personally, there are rules and procedures to deal with it all
> – occasionally bureaucracy can be helpful.

There is an important difference, though, between lecturers who generally expressed a belief in the efficacy and usefulness of centralized, university rules and those who placed more emphasis on self-chosen departmental standards. Some respondents were drawn from a culture that has a stronger tradition of university-wide regulation with respect to teaching and learning practices. These individuals were often, although not exclusively, lecturers based in post-1992 UK universities founded during the expansion of the higher education sector during the 1960s. Other respondents were more accustomed to developing rules and procedures within a departmental context on the basis of collective decision making in small teams or committees. This was more often the case with lecturers from 'older' university cultures. Thus, one version of 'abiding by the rules' relates to living with centrally imposed university-wide rules affecting teaching and assessment practices with which lecturers have had little involvement in developing. The other version, however, relates to a more collegial model where academics within the same department have had a say in collectively arriving at determining a rule or procedure. Hence, going 'against the rules' governing teaching and learning practices could be regarded as a failure to respect the principles of collegiality and an affront to colleagues in this latter interpretation.

However, the emphasis on following rules, either of university or departmental origin, was not a perspective shared by all respondents. For these lecturers, using their personal discretion and forming a judgement based on the individual circumstances of the student were as, if not more, important than following prescribed procedures. The focus of these lecturers was first and foremost on the individual and secondly on 'rules'. Unlike the 'absolutists', these lecturers were more 'situationist' (Forsyth, 1980) in their attitude to decision making. This difference was particularly well illustrated in the various assessment dilemmas that faced Dave Andrews (Chapter 5). Individuals who adopted a 'situationist' (Forsyth, 1980) stance were prepared to extend the deadline of the part-time, mature student depending on the exact nature of this person's particular circumstances. They were also more likely to recognize and make allowances for the possibility that plagiarism might arise owing to inexperience in referencing an essay or cultural differences. Their inclination was to resolve such matters informally with students rather than invoking the full range of rules and regulations. Negotiation is a more important tool for these individuals than a rigid insistence on rules and regulations.

A similar personal informality was the style recommended by situationists in dealing with other problems that arose in the case studies. They were more inclined to suggest one-to-one meetings with the disgruntled students who appeared in the case study in Chapter 7 and with the various members of staff involved. In the teaching observation, they also erred towards an informal but frank discussion between Stephanie and Max rather than an emphasis on including critical comment within a formal feedback sheet.

While inexperienced lecturers were inclined to emphasize the importance of following standard university or departmental procedures, staff with greater experience were more confident about seeking resolution using their own professional judgement (Macfarlane, 2002). In many respects, this finding is unsurprising, although it is interesting to speculate on the reasons why this should be the case. As suggested earlier in this book, newly employed university lecturers have been inculcated into a more rule-bound culture of university life. They are also, as junior academics, perhaps less confident about using their professional judgement in difficult situations. Although more experienced lecturers are more accustomed to exercising academic autonomy in decision making, there was disquiet expressed about what some perceive as an erosion of their professional decision-making powers. One of my respondents followed up her advice on the case studies with the following comment sent by e-mail:

> I was struck by how many of the ethical dilemmas raised in the case studies have been taken out of academic hands in my institution. There are 'procedures' for almost everything. This does make life easier and aims, at least, at equitable treatment. If the procedures are developed by relevant people, I suppose this is a good thing! But it does pose questions about the line between academic and administration functions and the proper areas of genuine discretion for academics.

The comment alludes to a perception that control of the procedures for managing student learning is being wrested from the hands of academics and into those of managers and administrators with little connection to the teaching context. As suggested in Chapter 1, the impact of a more bureaucratic and rule-bound environment is also related to rising student numbers in higher education. While it was relatively easy to adopt a more situationist approach with small student numbers and strong personal tutoring relationships, the time-consuming nature of this position becomes harder to sustain as student numbers rise. Certainly, individuals who have worked in higher education for many years with relatively high levels of personal autonomy appear to equate the notion of professionalism with freedom to make decisions affecting students unencumbered (as they may see it) by centralized administrative rules and procedures.

Emotion and distance

The importance of exercising 'emotional intelligence' (Goleman, 1995) has already been noted in relation to the case studies. This notion of emotional intelligence incorporates being aware of one's own emotions, learning how to handle these feelings, motivating oneself to achieve a goal, recognizing emotions in others and handling relationships effectively. All these aspects come into play as a teacher in higher education. Indeed, the importance of sensitivity was identified as a key virtue in relation to several of the incidents by respondents, although perhaps a more strictly accurate word for this virtue is empathy.

In dealing with the issues that confront Lesley Chung and Stephanie Rae in particular, a number of respondents argued that both of these characters were in need of staff or educational development which would improve their use of active and/or experiential methods. Such methods draw on the personal and life history events of students to improve interest, perceptions of relevance, understanding of the link between theory and practice and overall learning (Grauerholz and Copenhaver, 1994). Here it was suggested that a positive feature of good university teaching is to draw on the personal experiences of students and allow greater opportunities for learners to reflect on these in relation to learning. It was argued that this is an effective way of helping learners to make greater 'sense' of theory. In dealing with the confrontation in debate between two students, some respondents saw this as a lost opportunity for Lesley, as the teacher, to draw out the personal issues confronting these individuals in more detail. For these respondents, learning does sometimes raise uncomfortable, awkward personal issues which should not be side-stepped. This is as true for lecturers as it is for students. Hence, Max's lecturing style, despite an apparent imbalance, was praised by some respondents because it communicated his passion for his subject to the students (see Chapter 6). It was clear that Max was personally engaged by his subject and this, in turn, was more likely to stimulate an emotional response from students regardless of whether they agree or disagree with his standpoint. It was suggested that it may also be difficult for Max to teach in a more 'dispassionate' way. Brockbank and McGill (1998), for example, argue that teaching that seeks to hide personal perspectives is essentially inauthentic. Feelings will always leak out in the end. Thus, in the interests of motivating learners through displaying passion, and as a form of intellectual honesty, these lecturers saw a strong emotional engagement by the teacher as a positive feature of university practice.

Other respondents expressed a very different perspective in relation to the role of emotion in teaching. While they recognized the importance of using emotional intelligence and exercising sensitivity and empathy, they were less enthusiastic about bringing personal or emotional issues into the classroom. A small minority argued that the classroom is not the appropriate setting for discussion of personal or emotional issues. Their advice to Lesley, regarding the heated debate, was to speak to the students involved in the incident after the class and emphasize this very point. For these individuals there is a firm line between the 'academic' and the 'personal' and a suitable distance should be maintained between the two. More broadly, this may indicate a fundamental difference in perspective about the nature and purpose of a university education. For these lecturers, there is an important line in the sand between knowledge and personal experience. This attitude to the role of personal and emotional perspectives in teaching was also reflected in attitudes to Max's lecturing style. These individuals took Stephanie's position, expressing their own reservations about the potential (negative) effect of Max's passion on the academic freedom of students. They favoured an expository approach to lecturing, attempting to explain the issues in a balanced way, rather than adopting a didactic style which seeks to convince students of the efficacy of the teacher's view (Allen, 1988). The notion of presenting material as objectively as possible is an established feature of British academic life and, as such, this view may be, at least in part, a culturally bounded tradition.

While other respondents were not necessarily opposed to the importance of learning through reflection based on personal experience, several expressed qualms about whether lecturers are sufficiently equipped to deal with the consequences of encouraging students to engage emotionally as well as intellectually. Striking 'personal chords' was regarded as more likely once a lecturer stepped outside the discussion of theory and started to use problem-based approaches such as work-related scenarios, case studies or personal learning logs. Experiential learning is by its nature more unpredictable in the impact it has on learners. In similar vein to some of my respondents, Rowland (2000) explores the effect of encouraging emotional engagement in learning on academic staff undertaking a master's course in teaching and learning in *The Enquiring University Teacher*. In the book, Rowland describes one of his own workshops as 'in many ways more like a therapeutic experience than an academic one' (2000: 107). Rowland goes on to explore his own sense of disquiet on discovering that one of his course participants had reportedly found the workshop disturbing and had subsequently left the university suffering from depression. While Rowland's focus is on academic staff undertaking an educational development course, the observation he makes is equally relevant to teaching any group of students. In other words, should lecturers be encouraging students to unload their innermost feelings and thoughts? Is there a proper dividing line between 'teaching' and 'therapy'? Grauerholz and Copenhaver (1994) recognize the problem identified by Rowland. They put the dilemma more starkly by stating that, while there are pedagogic techniques which can help to protect the learner's identity and dignity while using experiential methods, there is always a danger to student well-being: 'We may be doing untold damage to our students by requiring or encouraging them to reveal difficult, perhaps traumatic, details of their lives in class assignments or classroom projects' (Grauerholz and Copenhaver, 1994: 321).

Certainly there is considerable support for the notion of keeping an appropriate 'distance' between the student and the teacher. Cahn, for example, argues that a teacher should 'not seek to be their (ie students') psychiatrist, friend or lover' (1986: 36). This is related to the notion that the *perception* of fairness must not be compromised in any way. The notion of appropriate 'distance' and perceptions of fairness encompass the widely held belief that teachers should avoid 'dual-role relationships' with students. Most obviously a dual-role conflict would occur where any kind of sexual or close personal relationship develops between the lecturer and the student. The Society for Teaching and Learning in Higher Education (STLHE) in Canada also warns against dual-role relationships based on familial, professional and business ties (Murray *et al*, 1996).

The spectre of a potential 'dual-role' relationship is hinted at only tangentially in one or two of the vignettes within the case studies. Here, there was a deliberate intention not to write a scenario, such as a sexual relationship between a student and a teacher, which could be easily condemned out of hand by respondents. The intention was also to avoid providing 'sensationalized' incidents and, instead, focus on more commonly occurring day-to-day incidents in the lives of lecturers. The newspapers, popular films and plays, such as David Mamet's *Oleanna*, provide a regular reminder of society's legitimate but somewhat narrow ethical focus on dual-role sexual relationships within university life. However, the 'persistent tutee' requesting additional support from Lesley Chung raises the possibility of either a dual-role relationship developing or being perceived to exist by other students and lecturers (see Chapter 4). Few respondents, though, as noted earlier, detected this possibility. Receiving a gift from a student is also censured by the STLHE in Canada in connection with dual-role relationships. The gift of a bottle of whisky to Dave Andrews from one of his students, however innocently intended, was widely seen by respondents as potentially compromising the lecturer's integrity (see Chapter 5). The vast majority suggested politely declining the offer. Even where it was suggested by some lecturers that the gift could be accepted, this policy was almost universally connected with a means, such as a charity raffle, of ensuring that transparency would avoid any perception or accusations of favouritism.

The encouragement of emotional engagement in learning by students also raises an issue connected to self-disclosure. The emotionally intelligent lecturer is, according to Mortiboys (2002), someone who is able to use disclosure of their own feelings or experiences to build a trusting relationship with their students. Self-disclosure is at the heart of learning that draws on the personal experiences of students but also relates to the power relationship between the student and the lecturer. There is a danger here that it is only the students who are being encouraged to self-disclose details of their innermost thoughts and personal experiences. This is potentially an abuse of the unequal power relationship between the student and the lecturer. As Grauerholz and Copenhaver comment, it is easy for lecturers to 'ask students to perform tasks that we would not be comfortable doing or we would not even be able to do' (1994: 323). In this kind of situation, teaching is in danger of turning into an exploitative form of psychotherapy by requiring students to recount their personal experiences but without the lecturer offering anything by way of a fair, emotional exchange of information.

While too little personal self-disclosure could be regarded as an abuse of the unequal power relationship where students are expected to reveal their personal experiences, the opposite is also potentially exploitative. In other words, lecturers who excessively self-disclose personal facts about themselves might be exercising too much emotional intelligence as a deliberate or inadvertent means of gaining the sympathy and good opinion of their students. Goleman (1995) uses terms like 'popular' and 'charming' to refer to people we tend to regard as emotionally intelligent. The phrase 'getting by on charm' can also imply an individual who uses his or her emotional intelligence in a manipulative way. This has the potential to result in the kind of halo effect in student evaluation of lecturers referred to in Chapter 6. In a recent and widely reported case, an award-winning US historian was accused of fabricating and aggrandizing his own personal experiences as a Vietnam war veteran and using these stories as a means of teaching his own courses on Vietnam and American culture. At one level, this well-publicized case is about straightforward accusations of academic dishonesty. At another level, it raises awkward questions about the extent to which other lecturers may be using exaggerated tales of their own experiences as a means of inspiring the interest and love of their students.

Conclusion

This chapter has discussed two important distinctions that have affected the way lecturers approach the decision-making dilemmas with which they were confronted in Part B of this book. To some extent these distinctions mirror the traditional characterization of the mind as having a 'rational' and an 'emotional' side (Goleman, 1995). On the rational side, lecturers understand the importance of sticking with universally applicable rules and maintaining emotional 'distance' from students to ensure that teaching decisions are made (and are perceived to be made) with objectivity. On the emotional side, lecturers are led towards the use of professional discretion on the basis of personal knowledge of the circumstances of the student and into forming deeper, more personally supportive relationships with both individual students and classes.

Here there is a tug-of-war taking place between the desire to engage emotionally with students and a concern to maintain a degree of distance as a way of coping with the power and responsibilities of professional life. It would be wrong to suggest that most lecturers stand in starkly opposed camps with respect to this dilemma. Rather, it would be more accurate to suggest that they recognize that such a dilemma exists and understand that part of being a teacher in higher education is about finding a way of negotiating this difficult balancing act. This highlights the need to avoid extremes of behaviour and find a 'middle way' based on fundamental virtues.

Chapter 9

Teaching with integrity

Introduction

The preceding chapter sought to explain the differences between lecturers in the manner in which they perceive or approach ethical dilemmas in professional life. By contrast, this chapter will reflect on the significance of the similarities. In offering their analysis, lecturers or my 'respondents', as I have called them, drew very similar conclusions in seeking to advise the fictitious characters over most incidents. The similarities in analysis offered are far more important to the essential purpose of this book in seeking to articulate what it means to teach with 'integrity' in a university setting.

The advice offered by my respondents has been converted in this chapter into a series of moral virtues for the modern university teacher. These, it has been argued, provide a more meaningful basis for professional life than anything that can be offered by a formal code of practice or good conduct guide. The shortcomings of this type of approach to the conceptualization of professional responsibilities were pointed out in Chapter 2. Rather, this chapter will argue for an alternative approach based on professional self-governance through the development of teaching virtues.

The word *integrity* has been chosen for very deliberate reasons, as first explained in Chapter 2. It refers to a concern to focus on the character of the actor rather than principle-based theories, such as utilitarianism or Kantianism. These theories can all too readily be converted into over-simplified decision-making templates. Rather than a 'rules and regulations' driven approach to ethical issues on campus, what is required is an identification of virtues compatible with reflective professionalism. This requires that the exercise of professional judgement is based on core moral virtues and conceived as a central duty of academic life. Some of the virtues (and vices) of the modern university teacher will be explored in this chapter.

The virtues (and vices) of university teaching

In Chapter 2, the reader was introduced to Aristotle's moral virtues, including justice, courage, pride and good temper. The continuing relevance of many of these virtues has become all too apparent through the analysis of the case studies. The virtues that emerge from this analysis are summarized in Table 9.1.

Virtues, as explained in Chapter 2, are median positions. They lie between extremes of behaviour or 'vices'. In this regard, it is clear, for example, that my respondents were opposed to the idea of a lecturer who experiments with teaching methods recklessly while, on the other hand, critical of those who lack the courage to consider introducing new techniques. Similarly, it is important for lecturers to adopt an open disposition in regard to the evaluation of their teaching. A lack of openness as a virtue might manifest itself in a defensive reaction to any criticism, while an excess of openness runs the risk of

Table 9.1   *Virtues for university teaching*

Virtue	Examples of application
respectfulness	in teaching students and in relations with colleagues
sensitivity	toward students seeking tutorial support; conducting peer review activities
pride	in adequate preparation to teach
courage	to innovate in teaching practice; confront challenging situations with students and colleagues
fairness	particularly in relation to assessment issues; investigation of complaints about colleagues
openness	in relation to self, peer and student evaluation of practice
restraint	in conveying the teacher's ideological and/or theoretical position; checking emotional reactions
collegiality	in managing courses and invoking consultative processes with students and colleagues

quiescence to the opinion of others, regardless of professional standards and personal beliefs (see Table 9.2).

The list of virtues emerging from the case studies reflects different aspects of personality. Pincoffs' (1986) analysis distinguishes between personality traits related to aesthetic qualities, such as wittiness, meliorating qualities, like even-temperedness, moral qualities, like altruism, and instrumental qualities such as resourcefulness. Clearly, some individuals will tend to possess more advanced 'mediating' virtues through tact, diplomacy and tolerance. Others are better at 'getting things done' through courage and determination. Here, there is a general distinction between non-instrumental and instrumental virtues (Pincoffs, 1986).

A higher education lecturer needs to possess a combination of instrumental and non-instrumental virtues. For example, to manage student and staff relationships successfully they require non-instrumental virtues such as sensitivity, openness and respectfulness. However, to bring about change both as an individual professional and a leader of others they need instrumental virtues such as courage and the cooperative virtue of collegiality.

Arguably, there are many other virtues relevant to being a 'good' teacher, such as wittiness, magnanimity and loyalty. Hence, it needs to be made clear that the analysis contained in this book does not purport to represent *all* the virtues of the 'good' university lecturer. It makes no claim to be comprehensive. The virtues identified are limited to the issues raised and debated in the case studies. Other case studies might, quite naturally, lead to the identification of other key

Table 9.2   *Teaching virtues and their vices*

Main area	Defect (vice)	Mean (virtue)	Excess (vice)
Teaching	disrespectfulness	respectfulness	over-protectiveness
Tutoring	indifference	sensitivity	favouritism
Preparation	complacency	pride	insularity
Innovation	cowardice	courage	recklessness
Assessment	arbitrariness	fairness	inflexibility
Evaluation	defensiveness	openness	quiescence
Ideology	evasiveness	restraint	self-indulgence
Managing	remoteness	collegiality	cliquishness

virtues. What follows, however, is a more detailed elaboration of the virtues (and vices) that emerged from the case studies.

Respectfulness

Class interaction with students formed the basis of incidents in Chapter 4 and is a crucial context for modelling the virtue of respect for learners. Creating conditions to facilitate discussion and debate in an open, tolerant environment was recognized as an important duty for any higher education lecturer. The ability of the teacher to create and maintain an environment where students feel safe enough to enter into discussion is both a pedagogic skill *and* an important virtue. There are discussion techniques that help to preserve the safety of the individual and also permit time for students to develop a more considered view before going 'public' in a whole-class context. However, such techniques can never entirely eliminate the possibility of the kind of exchange between Sam and Jane that occurred in the first case study (see Chapter 4). Here, it is crucial that the lecturer respects the students' right to self-expression, nurturing their sense of self-confidence and self-worth in the process. On the other hand, this should not imply that intolerant attitudes go unchallenged. This virtue needs to be developed and practised through experience in managing student discussion.

The unpredictability of class discussion is one of the joys of teaching but it also represents a reason why some lecturers fight shy of allowing adequate opportunities for students to express their views in this way. In allowing discussion to thrive, though, it is vital that students understand and respect the boundaries. If there are no 'ground rules' the result can be a free-for-all. At a mundane level, this may consist of students talking over each other, while, more seriously, this may lead to intolerant remarks that are of a sexually, racially or generally personally abusive nature. A teacher who fails to intervene in such instances becomes a silent party to such disrespectful comments. It is also clearly disrespectful for the teacher to make disparaging or sarcastic remarks about individuals, even where this is prompted by a sense of frustration at a lack of student preparation.

Knowing when to intervene to protect a student is important. Students need to be able to trust the teacher to protect them in class discussion by intervening when the boundaries are breached. On the other hand, students need to be given some latitude to debate issues without the lecturer constantly intervening. Thus, teaching interventions need to be limited and carefully judged since there is also a danger of being overprotective.

The classroom is a crucial context where the principle of procedural justice operates. Opportunities need to be afforded to all to contribute in some way. In this sense, lecturers act as arbitrators of time as well as the parameters of discussion. Individual students can sometimes dominate discussion and here it is crucial that the teacher strikes the appropriate balance between the rights of all individuals where, otherwise, discussion can become monopolized by one or two dominant voices. Being overprotective of a small, more articulate minority of students represents another extreme to be avoided.

Sensitivity

Despite the massification of higher education, respondents regarded sensitivity to the personal needs and circumstances of students as a core virtue. This word was used frequently by lecturers who studied the case studies. Learners, it was argued, should be treated as individuals with their own needs, ambitions and challenges rather than as members of an amorphous and faceless crowd. Being sensitive is a virtue that is closely related to the emotions. Although this was the term most often articulated by respondents, in many respects the word 'empathy' might more aptly encapsulate the essential need for lecturers to recognize and respond appropriately to emotions in others (Goleman, 1995). Empathy refers to this ability to understand the world from the other person's perspective. In using the term 'sensitive', respondents indicated both the need to project oneself into the 'place' of another and what Brockbank and McGill (1998) define as empathy-in-use: an ability to communicate this understanding to the other party. Moreover, the need for sensitivity was recognized in relationships with colleagues as much as with students.

This virtue emerged strongly in the context of the tutorial relationship, as explored in Chapter 4. Here, the core recommendation was to be sensitive to Brian's lack of self-confidence as a 'persistent tutee'. The sensitive lecturer should be concerned by the possibility that a variety of personal circumstances might help to explain Brian's behaviour. In other words, although Brian is seeking additional *academic* assistance, the root cause might be a *personal* problem. As one of my respondents commented, his persistence could be an indirect 'cry for help' unconnected with his academic work. Sending him away in a dismissive and unsupportive fashion would clearly be an insensitive response. Given the increasing diversity of students in higher education, it is possible that this student may not be as familiar with the demands of producing a traditional piece of academic work, such as an essay. As a consequence, he may need assistance from the lecturer or might be referred to colleagues working in student support or learning resources who have specialist skills in essay planning or researching academic sources.

Helping students to achieve higher academic standards is consistent with the commitment of all good professional teachers. Offering this or any other student unequal tutorial assistance, though, might be regarded by other students as unfair and undermine the legitimacy of the assessment process. There are also other dangers in being perceived to 'play favourites'. As discussed in Chapter 8, where dual relationships develop, or are perceived to exist, this can destroy the reputation of the lecturer as a legitimate authority. While the lecturer might be prompted by the purest of motives by seeking to improve the academic performance of a student, offering extra assistance might also encourage over-dependence on the teacher. It is widely recognized that university teachers need to wean students off an over-dependence on them as the source of all knowledge and wisdom. In this sense, the concern of the lecturer can potentially become suffocating for the personal and academic growth of the student. It can inadvertently fail to encourage the student to develop as a more self-confident and independent learner. While the goal of producing independent or 'lifelong' learners should not be taken as an excuse to curtly turn away a student such as Brian, there is a need for lecturers to strike an appropriate balance between the needs of the individual and fairness to the group in allocating out-of-class assistance. In this sense, ground rules are vital in the context of tutorial relationships.

As the vignette involving a tutee called Brian illustrates, a concern regarding fairness in assessment lies at the root of tutorial help with academic work. A tutorial relationship, though, is also about gaining a deeper insight into the personality and personal circumstances of the student. The knowledge gathered from the tutorial relationship should not be cast aside when confronted with particular incidents: the submission of a poor piece of work, a disappointing attendance record or, as illustrated in Chapter 5, the case of suspected plagiarism, the assignment extension requests and the offering of a gift. Here, even if the student is not well known to the lecturer, the role of individual differences should not be ignored. Respondents, for example, recognized the possibility that ignorance or inexperience might explain (although not necessarily excuse) the case of plagiarism and were more sympathetic if the students concerned were in their first year of study. Similarly, although lecturers were generally unsympathetic to those seeking an assignment extension on the basis of flimsy medical evidence, there was a sensitivity to the circumstances affecting many students in modern higher education. This applied both to the demands on part-time mature learners who have returned to study and to students with dyslexia who require additional support. Finally, different cultural norms and traditions were acknowledged as potentially explaining the offering of a gift of a bottle of whisky from a student from South East Asia. Again, the increased diversity of students means that lecturers need to exercise sensitivity to their different needs, backgrounds and personal circumstances.

Pride

While teaching continues to be widely perceived as a poor relation to research in terms of kudos and reward in academic life, the word *pride* encapsulates the importance of approaching this role with a conscientious attitude. Given the 'skewed' nature of current reward structures in higher education, a purely rational approach to seeking career advancement might exclude spending anything but the minimum amount of time in preparing, teaching, assessing and managing students. In Lesley Chung's case, there is a clear, underlying message from her Head of Department that she should get on with her research. If she spends a good deal of time preparing to teach a course which fails to coincide with her research interests, this is unlikely to advance her career. As one of my respondents commented, the added 'breadth' she needs to acquire to teach this course is different from the 'depth' of knowledge she needs to develop to research her subject. The demands lie in opposition.

However, teaching has traditionally been more associated with the intrinsic satisfaction it can give rise to rather than the material rewards we associate with modern career structures. Inspiring students, passing on the baton for a subject to a new generation, and seeing students gain in confidence and achieve success have always been more important to teachers than pounds, shillings and pence. This is not the same as saying that lecturers should be underpaid or exploited. However, it is sadly true that to 'get on' materially as an academic in higher education often means 'getting out' of teaching and moving into research or management. Despite the lack of material incentives, having pride as a teacher means caring about the student experience and keeping to one's own personal standards regardless of the lack of material rewards it may bring.

Although teaching and research interact in important ways, the dual responsibilities of the academic role, to teach as well as to do research, carry particular implications for this virtue. Teaching should not be disregarded as an unwelcome interruption to the business of research, a view assigned to Stephanie Rae in Chapter 6. Disparaging the importance of undergraduate rather than postgraduate teaching is an example of one of the 'taken-for-granted' practices in higher education identified by Knight (2002). This is a dismissive and complacent attitude that shirks an important professional responsibility. This attitude may also take the form of a failure to stay sufficiently up to date with the subject one is teaching, a particular challenge for lecturers in fast-moving and vocational areas of the curriculum.

Possessing a strong personal commitment to teaching carries different sorts of dangers. Few of my respondents recommended that Lesley completely overlook the writing of her academic paper in Chapter 4. While she should not ignore her teaching responsibilities, they also warned against a blinkered or insular attitude towards other elements of professional and academic practice, such as research. In this respect, Lesley's dilemma is typical of the kind of 'balancing' or 'juggling' act that modern academics need to perform.

Courage

The importance of courage as a virtue is one that respondents valued in a variety of contexts. They perceived courage as a preparedness to take difficult decisions, innovate in the classroom and seek continual improvement as a teacher. At one level, it has always been important for lecturers to be courageous enough to innovate and try out new ideas in their class. At another level, the importance of being courageous is very much a modern challenge. The changes which are currently affecting higher education, including massification and the increasing diversity of the student intake in terms of ability, background and culture, necessitate a re-examination of traditional teaching methods and approaches. This is as much an individual as a collective responsibility. Teaching a large, heterogeneous group consisting of the young and the mature, those with strong academic backgrounds and those with considerable work experience, those from the UK and abroad, is more of a challenge than lecturing a tightly homogeneous group of young, British-born students. It demands a degree of flexibility and a preparedness to take some calculated risks to improve the quality of the student learning experience.

The cowardly response to the changing nature of higher education is to carry on as if nothing has changed. At the organizational or departmental level this is the 'default' solution (Bourner and Flowers, 1997): simply teaching larger numbers of students through mass lectures and increasingly impersonal seminars. There is also, on a more general and personal level, a danger that lecturers will get stuck in the rut of habitual rather than reflective practice. It is tempting to stay in a 'comfort zone', relying on tried and tested material and lecture notes which have stood the test of time. Moreover, the lack of rewards associated with teaching mean that this is a rational temptation. Doing the 'rational thing' here means doing enough to get by rather than trying one's best, an attitude Simon has labelled 'satisficing' (Simon, 1957). In other words, it is not just the students who can display instrumental attitudes. It is a trap that lecturers can all too easily fall into as well.

In another context, being cowardly can also imply a failure to face up to or confront difficult issues. A number of my respondents were critical of some of the case study 'characters', especially Dave Andrews and Dilip Patel, for constantly putting off decisions and appearing to prevaricate. While this was a deliberate ploy, on my part, to encourage respondents to act as mentors in suggesting the decisions or actions that the characters should take, constantly sending students away or failing to speak with difficult colleagues is ultimately a failure of courage. This does not mean that knee-jerk reactions are preferable to deliberation and reflection. It does mean that eventually the buck has to stop somewhere and that while consulting colleagues and procedures are important it should not imply an abdication of responsibility to take difficult decisions when necessary.

The flip side of being cowardly is to adopt a reckless attitude. While university teachers now live in an environment in which innovation is being encouraged, partly in response to the pressing practical considerations of growing numbers of students entering higher education, this should not result in recklessness on their part. Dave Andrews, for example, was using a group assessment as part of his assessment strategy. What was unclear was the extent to which the implications of this form of assessment had been thought through. As the student group who came to see Dave protested, what is the strategy for dealing with free-riders? This is just one small example of the need to consider the consequences of innovation and to build in necessary safeguards to ensure that students are not inequitably treated as a result. In other words, experimentation in teaching should not be at the expense of the students who are being used as the 'guinea pigs'. There needs to be a careful consideration of the consequences.

Fairness

A core virtue, particularly in relation to assessment, is to be just or fair. One of the key differences, highlighted in Chapter 8, is between lecturers who emphasize dealing with assessment issues on a personal basis and those who favour strict adherence to university rules and regulations. Clearly there are dangers associated with both extremes of approach. Making decisions on an individual level runs the risk of inconsistency, leading to arbitrary decision making. A student's chances of gaining an extension for an assignment, for example, may end up depending purely on which member of staff the student seeks out. At the other extreme, a dogged insistence on sticking to the 'letter of the law' in every circumstance represents an inflexible mindset that fails to respond to exceptional personal circumstances.

It is clear that the concept of fairness or justice takes many forms (Chryssides and Kaler, 1996) and that these apply as much in the teaching context as any other. Procedural justice is concerned with how people should be treated in relation to rules that govern them. Decision making should not be arbitrary and procedures should be consistently applied. Giving someone a fair trial, for example, involves the case being based on the evidence, allowing both sides to put their arguments and following 'due process' in all other respects. Procedural justice has special resonance for university lecturers as a basis for exercising their professional role. There are a number of circumstances in which this principle is fundamental. The demands of procedural justice revolve largely, but not exclusively, around the assessment function. Is the grade fair? Has the process by which it has been arrived at been just? The requirement for student work to be

double marked is commonplace but the expansion of higher education means that larger teams of lecturers are now required to cope
with mass courses. This increases the difficulty and pressure in ensuring that assignments are marked fairly and consistently according to
common assessment criteria. Lecturers also play a crucial role in influ-
encing examination boards, where due process is essential. Here
lecturers are expected to act as impartial judges of academic worthi-
ness. Much of the discussion and concern that surrounds
staff–student affairs relates to whether academics in such relationships are able to maintain independence as examiners. This is at the
root of the dilemma concerning the offer of a gift to Dave Andrews.
Just the perception that the assessment process may have been
compromised puts the integrity of the entire system into question.

Fairness also demands the exercise of retributive justice or, in other
words, punishment for wrongdoing. Determining how to punish an
offence implies striking an appropriate balance between the extremes
of severity and leniency. Consistency is a key issue here that overlaps
with procedural justice. Punishing plagiarism is a prime example of
the power of retributive justice as exercised by lecturers and their
institutions. What is the proper punishment for plagiarism? The most
common punishment is to award a zero mark for the offending piece
of work (Parry and Houghton, 1996), but circumstances, and the exact
nature of the plagiarism, can vary greatly, ranging from 'sham para-
phrasing' to 'purloining' (Walker, 1998). Punishing plagiarism is part
of a wider disciplinary role that lecturers undertake. Perhaps the most
common example of this role is deciding on the appropriate punishment for the late submission of an assignment, another of Dave
Andrews' problems.

Remedial justice is best understood as the converse of retributive
justice. It is concerned with ensuring that the victim of an offence is
adequately compensated, or simply putting things right. Without
being too literal in applying this form of justice to teaching in higher
education, lecturers will be involved in a variety of decision-making
dilemmas where students are seeking restitution. Illustrations include
dealing with requests for coursework extensions based on illness,
family bereavement or other substantive, personal circumstances,
considering the merits of concessions and medical evidence at examination boards, or arbitrating in cases where students claim to have
been disadvantaged by other students in a group assignment. There is
now also a growing awareness in higher education of the individual

differences between learners and the disadvantages affecting some students. This raises questions regarding how students with 'specific learning difficulties' should be best helped. Students with dyslexia account for the largest and most rapidly growing group of disabled students in higher education (Pumphrey, 1998). However, controversy surrounds making concessions to students with dyslexia, especially where successful completion of their course of study may also entitle the student to practise as a professional (Morgan and Rooney, 1997). Students with other disabilities may require the services of assistants to act as note-takers, amanuenses or readers in order that they may be placed on an equal footing with other students. The assistant's role can cause controversy, though, when it develops beyond information collation into a tutorial relationship. Doherty (1996) reports that concerns were expressed that a scheme to provide disabled students with an assistant, initially paid for by the university, raised objections that the loosely defined nature of their role might result in recipients gaining an unfair academic advantage. This would break what Doherty (1996) refers to as the 'principle of equality'.

Finally, distributive justice relates to the morally correct distribution of things like wealth, power, property or obligations between individuals, and between and within groups and societies. It is a phrase closely associated with traditional socialist principles to redistribute wealth and ensure the provision of equal educational opportunities. The commitment of the UK government to encourage participation in higher education by under-represented groups is part of this agenda. At the pedagogic level, this principle relates to what have been termed 'allocation' dilemmas (Berlak and Berlak, 1981). In other words, how much time and attention should lecturers devote to individual students? One response to this question which many respondents expressed is that time should be apportioned equally. Some even quoted the use of standard tutorial allocations such as a maximum of 90 minutes per assignment for a postgraduate student. However, there are students who clearly enter higher education with fewer advantages than others in terms of ability, prior educational experience or both. This means that some students simply need more time and assistance than others. On the one hand, lecturers want to ensure that each student receives a fair share of their time. The fact is, though, that some students merit more attention than others. Hence, lecturers, like teachers in the compulsory sector, are caught in a difficult allocation dilemma (Berlak and Berlak, 1981). Here, as the responses to the various case study dilemmas illustrate, a balance needs to be struck, taking account of individual differences and needs while recognizing the importance of treating students on an equal basis.

Openness

Reflective professionalism demands that lecturers take a serious intellectual interest in the evaluation of their own practice. This involves being open to criticism from a variety of sources, including student evaluation, peer review and self-reflection. The principle underlying this virtue is that professionalism in teaching is in part characterized by openness of one's own practice and a willingness to share the products and processes of one's teaching with others. A commitment to continuous reflection and evaluation is one of the key values adopted by the UK's Institute for Learning and Teaching in Higher Education.

While it is easy to state that one is open to constructive criticism, this is a more difficult virtue to operate in practice. There is a natural human tendency to be defensive in the face of criticism, to dismiss derogatory remarks and refuse to face up to the truth. The unequal power relationship between students and lecturers makes serious consideration of criticism even harder. The lecturer is by definition the expert while the student is the novice. This makes the relationship far more complex than that of service provider and client. Stephanie Rae's reaction to the evaluation of her teaching carried out by students was a defensive one partly because the students were acting, perhaps inadvertently, as customers by 'benchmarking' her course unfavourably against those of her colleagues (see Chapter 6).

The formality of the evaluation process can also be a barrier to understanding and reacting effectively to student concerns. Part of Stephanie's problem is the sense of surprise and shock she feels at first reading the critical comments about her teaching. If she had involved her students in more informal, formative evaluation of her classes at an earlier stage she might have been more aware of student concerns and been able to respond less defensively. Another strategy she might have deployed would have been to treat the students as co-learners, to invite the students to set their own goals and be more open about the ways in which she, as the teacher, is still learning. This might have given the students a 'reality check' with regard to expectations and mutual obligations at the beginning of the course while also encouraging greater learner autonomy.

In conceptualizing evaluation of practice, though, it is important to recognize that students are not the only legitimate source of evaluation evidence. Account needs to be taken of self and peer evaluation and, where appropriate, the perspective of 'end-users' such as employers and professional organizations. Students are not the only party to the educational exchange with a legitimate view.

While defensiveness is a defective, if understandable response to evaluation, at the other extreme there is a danger of reacting in a quiescent or supine manner. This consists of being too prone to change practice in the face of criticism without engaging in a self-reflective process. It is an attitude that can be symptomatic of a lack of confidence on the part of the lecturer. It may also indicate that departmental or institutional evaluation procedures fail to place a value on self-reflection as part of the feedback process. In Stephanie Rae's case her students were critical of her use of peer assessment of oral presentations. One reaction to this criticism is simply to change the assessment of this assignment in the future. However, if Stephanie is genuinely committed to the use of peer assessment she needs to re-examine how the assignment was introduced to her students. Did they really understand the learning benefits? Were adequate safeguards used to ensure that the marking was fair? Responding to criticism is important but this does not necessarily imply abandoning key principles to which one is committed in the process. Student evaluation of Stephanie Rae's teaching benchmarks her practice unfavourably with that of another lecturer who makes lecture notes available on the Web. Although this practice is becoming more common in higher education, the rationale for providing lecture notes in this way needs to be thought through in relation to the teacher's objectives. It may represent an opportunity to devote more class contact time for active learning purposes but, in itself, represents nothing more than placing 'old wine in new bottles' (Saunders and Weible, 1999).

Restraint

Self-restraint is an important quality in any individual. It is also a fundamental requirement for professional life in forming trusting relationships with both students and colleagues. In the particular context of the case studies, the importance of this virtue arose principally in relation to a lecturer's ideological stance or commitment.

Lesley Chung has a passionate belief that economics should not be taught as an abstract science that ignores social and environmental issues, while Max Schaefer is a firm believer in 'letting students know where I am coming from' (see Chapter 4). It would be wrong to assume that ideological schisms and controversies are limited to disciplines from the arts and social sciences. They apply as much in statistics (Kruschke, 1998) as in psychology (Poe, 2000), although emotions, among both teachers and students, are most likely to be raised by discussion of so-called 'touchy' subjects or provocative claims connected with religion, sex, aggression, drugs, gender and ethnicity (Krushke, 1998; Poe, 2000).

Avoidance of difficult issues goes against the grain of academic and critical enquiry. The essence of academic life is closely connected with pushing the boundaries of new knowledge and questioning received wisdom. It is a critical attitude of mind which academics seek to develop in their students who, as the next generation of potential scholars, will help to carry the torch of intellectual advancement. Demonstrating a passion for one's subject is difficult, though, without sharing one's ideological and intellectual prejudices with learners. Indeed, emotion is a valuable tool for motivating students. However, as illustrated in Stephanie Rae's concerns regarding Max's lecture in Chapter 6, there is a danger that a passionate commitment to an ideological stance can result in a teacher becoming a domineering, rather than empowering, influence on his or her students. The perception of teacher 'bias' can result in student self-censorship, a concern raised by Stephanie Rae in the case study. While stating one's ideological position is consistent with an honest and open stance, to proselytize or indoctrinate takes advantage of the unequal power relationship between students and lecturers and can result in insidious effects on student freedom of expression. Restraint represents a median position between the extremes of denial that one has any ideological and/or theoretical position through to aggressive advocacy, regardless of the relevance to the teaching topic.

Respondents, though, did not favour being evasive with respect to an ideological position. In part this is connected with the principle of reciprocity. If students are expected to develop and practise their own arguments as junior members of the academic community, the lecturer has an obligation to reciprocate. This provides a basis for mutual respect within the context of the classroom, providing that students are reassured that they will not suffer prejudicial treatment if their reasoned intellectual stance differs from that of the tutor. Moreover, an academic who fails to give any clues about his or her ideological stance is probably less likely to be able to communicate a passion for the subject or help to motivate students in the process. There is a further attendant danger that a refusal to acknowledge explicitly an ideological position can result in an intentional or unintentional deceit whereby knowledge claims are presented to students as value-free, 'neutral' facts. There is a connection here between the notion of 'love' and 'distance' in the teaching relationship discussed in Chapter 8. Being frank and transparent with respect to one's own ideological stance will come more naturally to some lecturers than others, while maintaining an emotional distance from students is not consistent with 'baring your soul'.

Collegiality

Collegiality was defined broadly by respondents as consulting, discussing and taking joint decisions with academic colleagues and, on occasions, with students as well. It is also a concept associated by my respondents with supporting colleagues in the development and evaluation of their practice. The advice to talk to a more experienced or senior colleague was a dominant message throughout the feedback received. Sometimes, this can be a frustrating response to read or hear. It can often seem more like a 'cop-out', a refusal, in other words, by a respondent to face up to the situation themselves and offer an opinion rather than a piece of constructive advice. However, for the vast majority offering this advice it represented the importance of reflection and collaboration as part of the culture of academic life. Several respondents commented that individuals represented in the case studies appeared to be quite isolated. They were thrust into difficult situations and appeared to benefit from very limited support mechanisms. They were dissociated from their colleagues. The following comment by one of my respondents illustrates this particular point:

> It is significant that none of the imaginary lecturers perceive themselves as part of a wider academic or political community from which they can draw support or to which they can contribute. Their 'aloneness' is striking and politically significant. Their gut feelings are to consider the issues alone. They never think to go to discuss issues with a colleague, a mentor, or even a trade union representative at their university. They have no political sense of community.

As depicted in the case studies, this sense of community appears under threat in the conditions of higher education. Lesley Chung needs an understanding Head of Department, Dave Andrews needs a good mentor to help him with his assessment problems, Stephanie Rae needs the opportunity to discuss the critical feedback she has received with someone and Dilip Patel needs to improve communication and trust between all his colleagues. Underpinning the context of these case studies is the changing nature of academic life which has led to the current crisis of professional identity (Nixon, 1996). These changing conditions are characterized by an increasing emphasis on the assessment of the efficiency and effectiveness of higher education as a driver of economic change. In the UK, this has resulted in an expansion of the external audit of both teaching and research quality. One of the effects of this change has been a deepening divide between university 'management' and 'academics' (Walker, 2001). Although Dilip is an academic programme director, he stands at the cusp of this emerging divide. He needs to ensure that his colleagues conform to the rules and regulations of the university and that the programme he manages meets the demands of external audit. At the same time he needs to maintain their trust and respect as an academic peer. In this sense he is both an academic and a manager. It places him in an uncomfortable no-man's land between managerialism and collegiality, caught in the middle of one of the 'fault lines' or 'fractures' in academic life which divide academics from those that manage them (Rowland, 2002).

Collegiality, however, should not be confused with a cliquey indifference to the views and needs of students. It should not act as an excuse to ignore or dismiss the role of students as members of the academic community. For too long, lecturers in higher education have demanded the privileges of academic freedom for themselves while conveniently forgetting that students are also members of the academy who deserve the same protection. Furthermore, students have not traditionally been in a strong position to challenge the power of academics working within closely knit departments. The absence of a university ombudsman in the UK (although not in all countries) is symbolic of this historic lack of accountability. Despite the marketization of higher education, young and inexperienced students often do not possess the knowledge and confidence to be able to use mechanisms for accountability in an effective way.

Conclusion

This book has concentrated on the ethical responsibilities of university lecturers. It has not focused on the flip side: the duties of students. This does not mean that students do not share responsibility in respecting certain values as learners. These are often articulated in modern 'learning contracts' or 'learning partnerships' between academics and students. Common expectations of students include demonstrating respect for the teacher and fellow students, refraining from the use of intolerant and offensive language and abiding by the rules of the institution. There is much talk now about the shifting balance of power in the teaching relationship. Students are translating the values of consumerism into their expectations of university teaching. According to this thesis, the university is just another part of the shopping mall of modern consumer life. While this argument may be a slight caricature of the truth, student attitudes are changing and these have implications for the virtues that lecturers need to model.

To some extent the list of virtues summarized in this chapter are timeless ingredients of being a 'good' teacher. Virtues such as respectfulness, sensitivity or pride might fall into this category and they clearly have a lot in common with teaching in any context or phase of education from primary to post-compulsory education. Other virtues, though, also reflect the nature of what it means to be a modern higher education teacher in a more consumerist age. Openness in relation to the evaluation of teaching practice is a necessary element of 'reflective' professionalism in this less deferential environment. The availability of new technologies for teaching implies a willingness to innovate or seek some form of continuous improvement mediated by the need to justify the added benefits for learners. The changing nature and greater diversity of the student body also demand that lecturers respond in creative and flexible ways and have the courage to take calculated risks in response. Moreover, widening participation in higher education has added implications for the virtue of sensitivity, with students drawn from more widely varying social, economic, cultural and educational backgrounds.

Ethics in university teaching, though, as in all walks of life, is a complex business. It cannot be reduced to a simple checklist of solutions dictating right and wrong. As this book has argued, such rule-bound responses rob professionals of the essence of their professionalism: the ability to exercise judgement and engage as individuals with ethical issues. Making the right decision in complex circumstances is not an exact science. Lecturers, like other individuals, act principally on instinct, out of habit and, crucially, out of character formed on the basis of their experience and attitudes. In fact, as Richard Holloway argues in his book *Godless Morality*, ethics is a bit like jazz. It calls for a fluid approach in combining the best of tradition or the 'texts' with an open attitude to the current context: 'Morality is as much an art as a science and it calls for a certain versatility from us, the ability to improvise and respond to actual circumstances and particular situations' (Holloway, 1999: 16).

This does not imply, as Holloway argues, that anything goes. It means that it is important to strike a balance between the extremes of dogmatism and moral anarchy. In terms of teaching in universities it means recognizing the importance of basic moral virtues in forming relationships with students and colleagues based on trust and mutual respect. It also means that rational virtues such as a sense of fairness or justice need to be combined successfully with affective virtues such as sensitivity. The role of the university lecturer is still, in many ways, a privileged one in the exercise of power over the lives of students and comparative freedom to pursue intellectual lines of enquiry. These privileges, though, demand that considerably more attention is given to the development of the moral character of lecturers in higher education.

Chapter 10

Virtue under pressure

Introduction

A personal commitment to key virtues goes to the heart of what it means to teach with integrity. However, the political, economic and social conditions that frame professional practice in higher education determine whether lecturers find themselves working in a culture which largely supports or betrays these virtues. It is important to consider how personal commitment to the virtues of teaching fits within modern university culture. Hence, this final chapter will focus on the relationship between the virtue-based approach to academic professionalism outlined in the previous chapter and the broader context of higher education life. It will concentrate on the way key trends in modern higher education are shaping behavioural imperatives for universities and the academic communities they serve. The chapter will argue, in particular, that government policy initiatives in several countries in relation to massification, widening participation and auditing research quality have had a deleterious impact on professional virtues.

Massification and widening participation represent a social justice agenda few would contest in redressing the historic elitism of higher education. In the absence of adequate funding, however, such an agenda leads to a steadily worsening staff–student ratio. Evidence indicates that as a result of such unfunded (or under-funded) expansion in higher education, meaningful academic relationships between staff and students are undermined, together with the commitment (and practical ability) of some teachers to cope with the pastoral and scholarly needs of individual learners (Trowler, 1997; Jenkins *et al*,

1998). A second, significant trend is for governments to audit research quality in universities as a means of determining how to best channel funding connected with research. This has occurred in the UK, Australia, Hong Kong and elsewhere but has had a direct and often unfavourable impact on teaching. It has led, among other things, to the further concentration of prestige and resources in research activity and has had the effect of downgrading the status of teaching. Both under-funded expansion of higher education and research audit exercises have, I would argue, undermined commitment to a number of key moral virtues.

Roles in conflict

This book has been concerned with debating ethical aspects of teaching practice and the virtues they imply. However, the agenda that shapes the practice of teachers in higher education has long ceased to be determined by academics. Rather, the modern state, in the UK and beyond, controls both university finances and, as the 'piper who calls the tune', the ethical agenda to which institutions are required to respond. However, the reason for increasing state control of higher education is not entirely attributable to the steady rise in the proportion of public expenditure spent on universities since the start of the 20th century. According to Scott (1995), participation rates are more significant. In Britain, despite earlier expansions of the system in the 1960s, it was not until the mid-1980s that the percentage of students in higher education reached the benchmark figure of 15 per cent. The relative autonomy of the former elite university system gradually began to unwind as a result of massification (Scott, 1995).

While policy changes are now afoot to encourage institutional differentiation, in unitary systems of higher education, such as the UK, universities are formally equal in status and carry out roughly the same, multiple missions: teaching, research and 'service' to their local and regional communities. The role of academic staff tends to reflect this diversity and range of purpose. 'Service' is a term used to refer both to activities *within* the university, such as sitting on committees or acting as a student adviser or counsellor, and contributing to the wider community *outside* the university by giving public lectures, representing the institution on national professional associations and so forth (Knight, 2002). It is commonplace for academics, such as some of my own respondents, to talk in terms of this trio of responsibilities in describing their own work. However, the role of the modern academic is more complex than the rudimentary distinction between teaching, research and service may suggest. To convert 'research' into public recognition and influence successfully, for example, an academic must possess writing and networking skills. These are two of a number of key elements of successful academic practice, in addition to teaching, research and management of oneself and others (Blaxter, Hughes and Tight, 1998).

Boyer (1990) suggests giving renewed and reinvigorated meaning to the term 'scholarship', dividing academic work into distinct but overlapping scholarships of discovery, application, integration and teaching. Here, what is traditionally referred to as 'research' is redefined and incorporates the discovery of 'new' knowledge as well as attempts to apply existing knowledge to emerging fields of enquiry. Yet, even Boyer's definition of the academic role underestimates the importance of emerging aspects of practice such as curriculum design and innovation, management of students and colleagues, and the use of information and communication technology in association with teaching and the support of learning. The continuing gendered nature of academic life means that women are frequently expected, in practice, to contribute more in the service role, especially in relation to counselling students (Knight, 2002).

These attempts to reconceptualize and reclassify the nature of academic work are significant both in seeking to raise the status of teaching and in more clearly articulating the increasing role complexity of academic life. The multiple roles of the modern academic inevitably produce tensions. This increasing complexity, particularly in the context of multi-mission institutions, inevitably leads to role conflict. Academics tend to express a preference to spend more time doing research but at the expense of administration rather than teaching (Staniforth and Harland, 1999). In reality, despite attempts in recent years to redress perceptions of status, the commitment of academics to the teaching role is often the one that has come under the most threat.

The research imperative

The importance of being 'research active' to an academic is as much about self-identity and self-esteem as practical career survival and progression (Knight, 2002). The inequalities are so ingrained in terms of reward and recognition that the relationship between research and teaching in academic life has been likened to that of Adam and Eve in Milton's *Paradise Lost* (Badley, 2002). In any 'marriage' between research and teaching, it is clear who is wearing the trousers: 'Adam, the dominant, creative, male researcher married to Eve, the subservient, unimaginative, female teacher. Research is grandly reified; teaching remains a lowly process' (Badley, 2002: 445).

Thus, perhaps, the most significant role conflict that academics face is between the time they spend focusing on their research and all their other roles put together. This does not imply that the relationship between teaching and research cannot produce positive benefits. Indeed, ideally, teaching and research should provide the academic with a synergy of purpose and result in students learning with teachers at the cutting edge of their field. Mounting evidence, however, indicates that teaching and research functions are being pulled apart in the modern university, resulting in an increasing strain on the commitment of academics to teaching, and the virtues central to professional practice. While it is true that there have always been tensions between the teaching and research functions of academics, the situation has been exacerbated by government audit and funding arrangements for research.

In the UK, universities are funded separately for teaching and research. Government research funding of each university is determined by the quality of research undertaken, as measured by a peer review panel in each subject area, and the number of 'research active' staff. While superficially straightforward, the Research Assessment Exercise (RAE) has resulted in a range of time-consuming and costly activities by universities in an attempt to maximize their funding. So-called 'submission strategies' (Talib and Steele, 2000) have led to the commitment of extra resources to secure a higher research rating (and hence funding) by, among other things, releasing key staff from teaching duties to produce additional publications and the recruiting (or 'poaching') of research 'stars' from other institutions. Most damaging of all, however, is the creation of a 'them' and 'us' attitude amongst staff (Harley, 2002). This has been created by dividing lecturers into those who are 'research active' and those who are not, with the result that the latter group feel threatened, marginalized and inferior in status (Thomas, 2001). The pressure to publish in peer-reviewed journals in many subject areas has led to a loss of prestige for and interest in writing textbooks and ancillary materials essential to teaching

(Alderman, 2000). Staff producing the 'wrong sort' of research and publications, such as student textbooks, have been excluded from the selectivity process or pressurized into reorienting their efforts towards peer-reviewed journals instead. The RAE has also falsely raised the expectations of academic staff in formerly teaching-oriented departments and universities when efforts to increase research and publications output have not resulted in substantial additional funding. In short, the RAE, first introduced in 1986, has damaged the traditional unity of teaching and research in UK higher education and had a negative impact on a number of academic values central to teaching (Harley, 2002).

Although different in methodology, the Australian Research Quantum fulfils a similar function to the UK's RAE in determining research funding for universities. In this system, a Composite Index gives weightings to different types of publications such as edited books, refereed journal articles or doctoral theses supervised to completion. The Composite Index acts as a blunt instrument that pays no regard to disciplinary differences in publication patterns. While the Composite Index has been adjusted since its introduction in the light of criticism, it still distorts the research output of staff under pressure to maximize institutional performance and commensurate funding. Again, the overall effect has been to elevate the importance of research productivity at the expense of teaching (Harman, 2000).

The case studies in this book included examples of the role conflict of the modern academic with particular reference to when teaching and managerial responsibilities collide with personal research agendas. In Chapter 4, Lesley has to make a difficult choice between adequate preparation to teach a new course and completing a paper for publication. In Chapter 7, Dilip is doing more 'service' (course management, in this instance) at the expense of his research. Here, several respondents were quick to recognize these dilemmas. In Lesley's case, comments from respondents included:

> There is a conflict here between her integrity as a teacher (prepare fully) and her integrity as an academic (carry on with her research). But the 'management' has given her a clear guide on this (carry on with her research).

> My advice would be; teach the subject, do enough to get by and get on with your research.

In Dilip's case involving multiple student complaints and apparently uncooperative colleagues, other respondents remarked:

> Unfortunately in most universities there are no prizes and little kudos for patience and thoroughness in dealing with this sort of thing, even where there are prizes and rewards for (other aspects of) excellent teaching.

> Within a properly collegiate system all elements of the academic role (research, teaching, administration, tutoring) would have equal weight. For instance, someone can thrive in research only because they are supported by colleagues in their department who are slogging away at teaching and tutoring. This cooperative dimension of academia is today constantly under threat – in part by the inappropriate stress on research.

As the final quotation makes clear, reward on the basis of a narrow definition of research has had a corrosive effect on dispositions of collegiality. Other virtues, identified earlier in this book, are also under threat. The virtues of pride and sensitivity demand that teachers spend adequate time preparing lectures, writing and updating learning materials, advising and counselling students and giving meaningful feedback on assessed work. Evidence indicates that, under a growing pressure to research and publish, 'corner-cutting' measures are degrading the student learning experience. Common strategies to claw back time for research include dropping coursework in favour of a single examination, tight restrictions on student access to dissertation supervisors, reducing the number or increasing the size of seminars, and using inexperienced postgraduate students in place of research-active lecturers (Gibbs, 2002). Sadly, reducing staff–student contact time is a common goal that drives many e-learning initiatives both at institutional and departmental level.

This is a depressing picture of teaching devalued and comparatively poorly rewarded. In many ways, this is hardly a new phenomenon for which government funding initiatives are uniquely responsible. It needs to be recognized that there have always been tensions between teaching and research, making these functions conflicting, rather than mutual, dimensions of the academic role (Fox, 1992). Perhaps a more positive way forward here is provided by the approach to research assessment adopted in Hong Kong in 1999. Here, rather than focusing purely on the audit of traditionally defined 'research' activity, Boyer's (1990) categories of scholarship were adopted as a basis of assessment. Discussions led to the recognition of high quality case studies and course materials which were 'truly innovative, generalisable, publicly accessible and peer-reviewed' (French, Massey and Young, 2001: 39). The business of arriving at a shared understanding of 'what counts' as scholarly outputs in the Boyer categories of integration, application and teaching has clearly some way to go. There are grounds for hope, though, that a more inclusive and less divisive system of auditing scholarship will redress the current imbalance which undermines the basis of key virtues such as a collegial disposition, pride and sensitivity.

Role overload

The current participation rate in English higher education of those aged between 18 and 30 is approximately 43 per cent (DFES, 2003). The UK government is committed to raising this figure to 50 per cent of the relevant population by the year 2010. Moreover, this is a trend reflected elsewhere in the world. The Dawkins reforms led directly to a 40 per cent increase in the participation rate in Australia between 1989 and 1992 (Layer, 2002). The participation rate elsewhere is considerably higher, such as in New Zealand and in the Scandinavian countries of Sweden and Finland. In the UK, there were significant increases in the participation rate both in the late 1960s and, more latterly, from 1988 to 1993 (NCIHE, 1997). Indeed, between 1991/92 to 1994/95 the percentage of young people entering higher education rose from 23 to 32 per cent (Watson and Taylor, 1998).

The reality of modern higher education in the UK, as in many other countries, is that of a mass system. However, much of this expansion has been inadequately funded. Watson and Taylor (1998) estimate that in the 15 years prior to 1998 the unit of resource available to universities and colleges of higher education has fallen by roughly 40 per cent. The impact of this under-funding can be seen in deteriorating staff–student ratios, larger classes and reduced contact time for students with their teachers (NCIHE, 1997). Workload and stress levels are acknowledged to have increased as a result of a range of factors but with the core reason attributable to much larger student numbers.

On the face of it, widening participation in higher education is a laudable goal. By making higher education inclusive, rather than an exclusive experience, it promotes social equality both for members of traditionally under-represented socio-economic groups and disadvantaged minorities, such as people with disabilities or those living in rural and remote areas. It means that universities become better aligned to the needs of the communities and societies they serve. Widening participation is especially important in the context of less-industrialized countries, such as the case of South Africa in the post-apartheid era (Scott, 2002). While the motivation of governments to widen participation may also be attributable in developed countries to the need for highly skilled human capital in a post-industrial age, social justice is served in the process (DFES, 2003).

However, increasing participation rates in higher education have rarely been associated with a commensurate rise in the resources needed to fund such expansion. In the UK, the proportion of GDP spent on higher education actually fell between 1995 and the year 2000 from 1.29 per cent to 1.13 per cent (Watson and Bowden, 2000). Indeed, during a period of rapid expansion in student numbers between 1989 and 1997 funding per student dropped by 36 per cent (DFES, 2003). Quite simply, for teachers in higher education, ever-growing numbers of students have not been accompanied by the resources necessary to maintain teaching and tutoring relationships, thereby resulting in reduced opportunities for lecturers to offer students individual support (NCIHE, 1997).

In a British context, Scott contends that the 'emphasis on the privi-leged (even private) character of student–teacher exchanges, a strong belief in pastoral intimacy...' (1995: 23) are characteristics of an elite higher educational past. Yet, the preservation of a meaningful personal relationship between a student and a teacher cannot simply be dismissed as an elite instinct. Rather, it goes to the heart of what it means to be a teacher; helping individuals to learn. Massification, in any context, runs the risk of alienating students from teachers and leaving lecturers feeling isolated (Shils, 1982). While massification means that more young people experience a university education, it is associated with higher attrition or 'drop-out' rates both in the UK and in the United States (Nelson and Watt, 1999). By US and some European standards, drop-out rates in UK higher education have traditionally been low. By the end of the 1990s, though, this reputation was under threat, with some universities reporting attrition rates of over 40 per cent. Attrition rates are attributable to a wide range of causes, including student poverty. It is also probably, at least partly, attributable to the erosion in contact time between staff and students.

The literature now abounds with pragmatic advice and suggestions as to how teachers in higher education should adjust their teaching methods to cope with mass student numbers. While these may be cost-effective solutions, rather less attention is paid to the implications of maintaining meaningful teaching and pastoral relationships with students. Both officially designated personal tutors and teachers known to students whom they find approachable have historically played a significant role in supporting students in a variety of ways as, among other things, being a friend, adviser, referral agent, advocate, counsellor, teacher, referee and confidant (Blaxter, Hughes and Tight, 1998). Moreover, the need for this type of personal support is especially acute given the additional needs for tutorial guidance of students from previously under-represented groups in higher education, such as those from economically disadvantaged backgrounds or with disabilities. While most teachers in higher education would endorse the goal of widening participation in principle, in practice they face a professional and ethical crisis trying to ensure that they respond adequately to the needs of each individual student. The ideal professional paradigm is to be able to cope with both demands:

> The kind of professional paradigm we are trying to imagine would both privilege the student–teacher relationship (particularly small discussion and tuition) and open up access through an increasingly varied further and higher education sector, catering for people of all ages and in different circumstances. (Nixon, 2001: 239)

Thus, the 'essential conundrum' (Nixon, 2001: 239) faced by teachers in higher education is how to support widening participation initiatives while maintaining their own professional standards of responsiveness to the needs of individuals in the process. Massification has occurred not just in the UK but in Australia and many other countries across the world without the funding to match the expansion in student numbers. To some extent, this phenomenon represents an abuse of the trust between university lecturers, the institutions for whom they work, national governments and, last but not least, the students they serve:

> Teachers might also be trusted by the institution to fulfil the grandest of mission statements, yet work in the full knowledge that these are simply marketing devices which cannot be attained in an environment characterized by individualism and competition. (Curzon-Hobson, 2002: 273)

While nearly all university lecturers are sympathetic to government and institutional values which emphasize the need for greater access and wider participation, they find that their commitment to personal and professional virtues which emphasize responsiveness to the needs of individual students is threatened as a result. Work overload as a consequence of rising student numbers, among other factors, means that academics deploy a variety of coping strategies (Trowler, 1997). The deleterious effects of rising student numbers accompanied by deteriorating staff–student ratios on teaching are, in many respects, similar to those identified earlier in relation to the impact of the research imperative. These include failing to update teaching notes, speed marking of assignments and, most concerning of all, deliberately making themselves 'unapproachable' as a means of reducing demands placed on them by considerably larger student numbers (Trowler, 1997). Studies also indicate that academic staff now spend significantly less time in general teaching preparation (Talib, 2001). Reducing student access to staff is also a response closely connected with the impact of demands for increased staff research (Jenkins *et al*, 1998). Students will tend to approach teachers whom they find more friendly and accessible (Blaxter, Hughes and Tight, 1998). Making oneself deliberately 'unapproachable' damages trust with students and represents an abdication of shared responsibility with more 'accessible' academic colleagues.

It is clear that a number of academic departments either tacitly or explicitly endorse such responses to rising student numbers and pressures to increase research productivity. Departmental strategies include drastically reducing the number of hours staff teach (Coate, Barnett and Williams, 2001). Such tactics are often linked to the anticipated benefits of electronic learning, although, in reality, conscientious teachers find that the demands of managing asynchronous activities, such as student discussion boards, make equal if not greater demands on time than traditional methods (Postle and Sturman, 2000). The casualization of academic labour over recent decades via part-time, short-term and casual employment practices also has adverse implications for the development of teaching relations. In the United States it is estimated that only about a third of the teaching is carried out by tenured staff (Nelson and Watt, 1999). Although employing casual labour may make economic sense and release full-time, tenured staff from teaching duties, it also further impoverishes the student experience unless justified on the grounds that such staff bring special expertise, such as a contemporary perspective from a professional or clinical context.

While measures to reduce contact hours between staff and students are understandable in the context of funding regimes and other institutional constraints, they have a corrosive effect on a number of key virtues, such as sensitivity, pride and a collegial disposition. Moreover, the environment within which university teachers practise has a significant impact on the virtues that teachers will develop. Junior members of staff, especially, will take their lead from more senior faculty. Virtue is learnt through the observation of good examples set by others who, knowingly or unknowingly, act as role models (Ryle, 1972). University, departmental or faculty cultures which respond pragmatically to system-wide pressures need to assess the potential long-term damage to professional integrity that this may cause.

Future directions

This book has sought to promote an integrity-based approach to teaching in higher education rather than a conceptualization of ethics based on a compliance and rule-bound model. The same approach is overdue in relation to research. The world of 'research ethics' is dominated by codes of conduct, professional and academic associations and university ethics committees whose task is essentially a negative one: to prevent unethical research conduct. Codes of conduct provide a 'top-down' approach to ethics which tends to accord an exaggerated importance and privileged status to the claims of particular ethical theories (Small, 2001). More often than not, the Kantian principle of respect for persons is enshrined in codes of research conduct. Unfortunately, such codes are concerned with an essentially regulatory agenda in seeking to define what constitutes misconduct and how this may be prevented (Grinnell, 2002). Commonly they insist on obtaining informed consent and maintaining the anonymity of research subjects, principles I have sought to respect in writing this book.

These codes, however, like those drafted in relation to teaching, contain the same systemic shortcoming: when faced by complex situations and conflicting rules, how should one act? For example, is it really possible to research adequately the underlying causes of football hooliganism without concealing one's identity and becoming a member of the 'tribe'? Gaining access to conduct research in business organizations can be problematic and lead to pressure to compromise the confidentiality of workers as a *quid pro quo* (Easterby-Smith, Thorpe and Lowe, 1991). Ultimately, the only real 'answer' to the question of how one should act can be found in developing individuals with a *disposition* to act appropriately in any given situation (Pring, 2001). What is required, in other words, are good people who possess moral judgement. This applies as much in research as it does in teaching. Pring (2001) articulates the virtues of the educational researcher in the following terms:

> The moral virtues would be those concerned with the resistance of the blandishments or attractions which tempt one from the research, even where the intellectual virtues press one to go on; courage to proceed when the research is tough or unpopular; honesty when the consequences of telling the truth are uncomfortable; concern for the well-being of those who are being researched and who, if treated insensitively, might suffer harm; modesty about the merits of the research and its conclusions; humility in the face of justified criticism and the readiness to take such criticisms seriously. (Pring, 2001: 418)

Clearly, from Pring's exposition, the moral virtues of a 'good' researcher share much in common with the 'good' teacher in higher education. They are excellences of character which go to the heart of researching with integrity. The environment in which research takes place plays the same critical role in this sphere of academic practice as in teaching. Again, as I have argued in relation to teaching, without a supportive environment the commitment to personal virtue in research is likely to weaken (Pring, 2001).

Conclusion

Despite the multifaceted and demanding nature of academic life, a deepening role conflict and the damaging effect of government policy initiatives to audit research quality and expand participation without adequate funding arrangements, teachers in higher education still cling to a keen sense of personal obligation to the individual student. However, this sense of duty is increasingly under pressure, as the following letter, written by a retiring UK academic, serves to illustrate:

I am ready to retire at 65 at the end of this academic year. I am gasping for the moment. There are now half as many full-time members of staff in my subject area than there were six years ago with at least a third more students. We no longer have time for innovative work let alone research. The increasing administrative and pastoral responsibilities make teaching of, and mutual learning with, students impossible. (Bob Bennett, 2002)

Fortunately, there are still grounds for optimism. Most academics do not operate purely on the basis of a rational calculation of personal 'profitability' (Knight and Trowler, 2000). Such calculations would persuade the rationally minded to focus on their research and publication record and overlook the obligations of the teaching role. 'Busy' academics still find time for their students despite the pressures they face (Coate, Barnett and Williams, 2001). While teaching may not be the most favoured activity of all academics, it is an essential element in the identity of a university lecturer.

The pressures that academics face in coping with the twin demands of rising student numbers and research productivity are a clear threat to virtue. They perhaps demand possession of a final virtue, that of a generosity of spirit or an individual disposition to spend time helping individual students, preparing learning and teaching materials, giving feedback, writing references and many other time-consuming but materially unrewarded aspects of university teaching. Despite the pressures they face, the academic community does have a shared vision of the moral virtues appropriate to teaching. Encouraging their discussion and practice is probably the best way of ensuring that the forces that threaten to erode commitment to virtue are kept at bay.

Appendix

The case studies

The University of Broadlands

The fictional institution represented in the case studies that follow is The University of Broadlands, an institution founded in the UK in the 1960s as a broadly vocationally oriented 'polytechnic' but which, since 1992, has been reclassified as a university. Since 1992 the university has sought to increase its reputation for research. There is a student population of about 20,000 of whom around 70 per cent are under-graduate students enrolled on a wide range of degree programmes in the Arts, Humanities, Health and Social Sciences. These contain a range of professional and vocational degrees in addition to more traditional subjects such as History and English.

All of the individuals referred to in the case studies are figments of the author's imagination and do not refer to any living person.

Case study 1: Teaching

Dr Lesley Chung has worked as an Economics lecturer at The University of Broadlands for the past 10 years. She went part-time for 18 months three years ago after starting a family, but recently returned to a full-time position at the university. Lesley was previously employed at a neighbouring university as a research assistant where she completed her doctorate in environmental economics. Subsequently, although she has sustained a keen interest in social and environmental analysis within economics, she has found it increasingly difficult to keep up her research and publications. The demands of teaching and administration, coupled with responsibilities as the primary carer for her young son, have made it difficult for her to find the time to publish, although the Head of Economics sees research as 'the department's number one priority'. Her work mainly consists of teaching Economics to first-year undergraduates.

Lesley's teaching commitments include a number of regular weekly seminars in first-year Economics to groups of between 15 and 20 students and tutorials to individual students. She also teaches her own specialist module in Environmental Economics to second-year students, depending on demand. Seminars are used within the department to follow up on lectures, with an emphasis on student-led analysis and discussion. Thinking back over what happened during today's seminar, Lesley does not feel entirely happy. Two incidents occurred which are now worrying her.

The first incident happened close to the start of the seminar session. The students had seemed to be in good humour, perhaps because the end of term was drawing near. As usual, she had spent the first 10 minutes or so of the seminar recapping on some of the key concepts discussed the previous week. Lesley found this a useful way of checking that the students had done sufficient reading and worked through exercises in the course text following the lecture. It was also a two-way process where students could ask Lesley to clarify concepts they were unclear about. There was a light-hearted atmosphere at the start of the seminar and it became clear to Lesley that not enough work had been done in preparation for today's class. After a series of unsatisfactory answers to questions, one student made a particularly inept response at which point Lesley said, sarcastically, 'Clearly you've left your brain at home today! Can anyone else provide a meaningful answer to the question?' There was a ripple of laughter followed by an awkward silence. After a few seconds one of the brighter students in the seminar answered the question in a satisfactory way and the discussion moved on.

Lesley believes passionately that economics should not be taught as an abstract science that ignores social and environmental issues. In today's seminar she had arranged for a structured discussion of government 'macroeconomic' priorities on the basis of two articles and a short video shown to the group. At first this stimulus material had worked well, leading to a lively debate with a series of good points being made, including the interdependence of national economies. Unfortunately, an incident occurred during discussion, which is now causing Lesley to ponder. She had tried to draw out one of the quieter students, called Sam, who had previously been too shy, it had seemed to Lesley, to make an oral contribution in class. Things got heated, though, when he had said, 'Friedman's right. Getting inflation down is much more important than unemployment. That will sort itself out in the long run.' However, this remark resulted in a terse and angry retort from another student, called Jane: 'Extremists like you make me sick. You wouldn't say that if your father had been unemployed for the past 8 years.' The sharpness of this exchange took everyone by surprise, but after an uncomfortable silence of a second or two the discussion exploded back into life, with several students contributing in rapid succession, although Sam did not take part. The difficult moment had passed but Lesley was left wondering then and again later, on reflection, whether she should have intervened at this point. She had hesitated to intervene at the time, she recalled, because she sensed from Jane's terse reply that she was speaking about how unemployment had affected her own father. Perhaps she had also not intervened because she felt broadly supportive of Jane's view. She was not sure whether she had done the right thing to say nothing or let the incident go as part of the general 'cut and thrust' of classroom debate.

While thinking about the incidents in class earlier in the day, there was a knock at her office door. It was Brian Stevens, yet again. He had been to see Lesley at least three or four times recently about a final coursework essay due in next week for the Economics course. While Lesley had made it clear to the class as a whole that they were welcome to see her for a tutorial about their essays, as usual, few had taken her up on the offer. This had been a relief in a way, given her workload and problems sharing an office with a colleague. However, Brian had seen her for an initial discussion about sources, a second time to talk through the essay titles and on two further occasions with different essay plans. He was a bright and conscientious student who had done well in his previous assignments but basically seemed to lack self-confidence. This time he had brought along an essay draft and asked whether Lesley could have a quick look at it to let him know whether he was 'going in the right direction'. To Lesley, it looked more like a near-completed essay than a 'draft'. It came as a welcome relief when the telephone rang, giving Lesley the opportunity to ask Brian to return during her next scheduled 'office hour' the following day. She was in a quandary, though, about what to do about Brian's request as he was bound to return tomorrow.

The telephone call had been from the Head of Department confirming the bad news that insufficient student numbers had opted for Lesley's Environmental Economics option in order for it to 'run' next term. Instead, to make up her teaching hours, Lesley would be expected to take the Economics of European Integration option. Lesley was disappointed about not being able to teach her specialist area and had mixed feelings about teaching the Economics of European Integration, an area she had little real interest in which drew heavily on international trade theory. While she had taught this option a few years ago, filling in for a colleague who had been on study leave, she felt pretty rusty in this specialist area. Looking at her notes, a little later in the day, she thought she had probably got enough to 'get by'. If she did not spend too long in preparing to teach the module she might even be able to finish a research paper which she had been trying to complete for more than 8 months now. Besides, she had heard a rumour that the department would be advertising for an international trade specialist for the beginning of the next academic year and probably he or she would take over the teaching of this option anyway from next academic year.

Case study 2: Assessment

It is Dave Andrews' first term as a lecturer in Sports Science at The University of Broadlands and he has been finding it hard going. After spending most of his twenties doing a PhD and then working as a postgraduate research assistant on various projects, Dave secured a lectureship on a three-year contract last September. Although Dave did 'pick up the odd seminar' while working as a researcher, he started his new job with very little teaching experience. He was shocked that as a new lecturer he was given such a heavy teaching load and feels dumped with several irksome administrative jobs, such as 'quality assurance', which clearly no one else in the department wants to do.

Today Dave has a busy day ahead, with teaching in the morning and the afternoon. He desperately needs to finish marking some assignments which he has promised to return to the students by the end of the week. He also has a scheduled 'office hour' at lunchtime in order that students can come to see him on a first-come-first-served basis. Dave returns to his shared office after finishing his morning teaching. It is now his office hour but he decides he needs to get on with his marking.

Before he can get very far, though, there is a knock at the door and three students enter. They want to talk to him about a group presentation, an assessed part of their course, which they are due to do next week. Dave listens while the three students tell him that the fourth member of their group has hardly ever turned up for meetings to discuss the presentation and is generally not 'pulling his weight'. The students say they have done a lot of work and are worried that the fourth group member 'will just turn up and take equal credit for all our hard work' on the day of the presentation. On the other hand, they are also concerned that their grades will suffer as the fourth group member has not prepared properly. They ask whether they can do the presentation without the fourth member. Dave tells the students that he will have to think about it and sends them away with a promise to see them the next day.

Munching a sandwich, Dave returns to his marking but quickly becomes concerned about two essays which appear very similar. On closer inspection Dave notes that there are whole paragraphs which are almost identical save for the odd word or different phrase in places. He remembers that the two students had worked well together on an earlier group project and are probably good friends. Dave sighs and puts the two essays to one side. He will have to think about this.

Just as he is about to mark another essay, there is a knock at the door and a student enters looking somewhat sheepish. The student explains that he feels under a lot of pressure because he has a number of assignments due in at the same time. He also mentions that he had a cold last week. The long and the short of it is that he wants an extension on the essay set more than two months ago at the beginning of term. The telephone rings and Dave tells the student to come back in the morning to discuss the matter further.

After finishing his last teaching session, Dave returns to his office and remembers that he had better check his e-mail. Dave opens two messages from students. Opening the first e-mail, he recalls that this student is attentive and a good attender, although he is yet to mark any of her written work. The e-mail explains that as a dyslexic student she would like a few days' extension on the assignment deadline in order that it can be checked over for errors by an adviser at the Student Learning Centre (a central body at Broadlands which, among other things, helps students with learning difficulties). The other e-mail is from a mature student Dave teaches on a part-time postgraduate course. This student also wants an extension, citing 'work pressures'. Both of these requests for an extension relate to the assignment set more than two months ago at the beginning of term. Dave decides not to reply immediately to either e-mail in order to think over the requests before making a decision.

Half an hour later the departmental secretary appears at Dave's office with a gift for him left in the departmental office by a Chinese student from Hong Kong. The present, wrapped in Christmas paper, turns out to be a large (2 litre) bottle of whisky (Dave's favourite tipple is single malt and he remembers, somewhat guiltily, how he made some light-hearted reference to this effect, as an aside, at his last lecture). The card reads: 'To Mr Andrews, my favourite teacher, Merry Christmas and a Happy New Year, thank you for all your help, best wishes, Lee'. Dave recalls that this is a hard-working student but one who has struggled to gain good marks, partly due to problems with written English. Ironically, Dave has Lee's latest assignment as the next one on the pile to mark. He wonders what he should do about the bottle of whisky.

Case study 3: Evaluation and review

Professor Stephanie Rae entered her room and let her stack of papers and books hit the desk with a satisfying thud. Reclining in her chair, she felt an overwhelming sense of relief. She had finally seen the back of the postgraduate research methods course for the term and could now get back to her 'real' work, as she saw it, by concentrating on a major new research grant proposal. The students had not been an easy group this year.

Stephanie had been appointed as a Professor in Health Sciences at The University of Broadlands four years ago, having established an international reputation for her research work into evidence-based health care. Her busy professional life left her little time for other things, although Stephanie had always been a committed member of the Church of England. The research methods course was her only formal teaching commitment in addition to master's and doctoral supervision. Much of the rest of her time was spent working on various research projects, speaking at conferences, writing for publication and editing a major journal in her specialist field. However, although she had just finished teaching the research methods course, there was the little matter of the student evaluation questionnaires to consider. Sitting at her desk, Stephanie started to skim casually through the questionnaires which she had collected from the students at the end of the last session of her course. Departmental and university procedures required staff to evaluate their teaching and Stephanie's department used a standard questionnaire for all postgraduate courses. Lecturers (and professors!) are expected to collect this information, have the results analysed and include this in their annual course report. While she could give these evaluations to one of the department's administrators to analyse, she usually felt a little embarrassed about letting someone else see them.

Reading the comments of her students, Stephanie became increasingly concerned. There were positives but quite a few complaints about 'boring readings' which were 'too theoretical'. There were also unfavourable comparisons made between Stephanie's approach and the way another, more junior colleague made lecture notes available on the Web and provided handouts of lecture slides in advance. Stephanie, though, had qualms about 'spoon feeding' the students in this way. There were also irritatingly low 'scores' from a minority of students who claimed not to understand the assessment process even though she had explained at length the role of this process in the course handbook. They were probably, Stephanie guessed, poor attenders who had got a low mark in their first assignment, a project proposal. Finally, following a teaching observation carried out by a colleague the previous term, she had tried to be 'innovative', with the encouragement of the university's Educational Development Unit, by getting the students to assess each other during oral presentations of research project outlines. However, several of the students complained that they were fed up with being used as 'guinea pigs' or being 'experimented on'. One student commented that 'Lecturers are paid to assess our work. Why on earth should we do it!' Momentarily, Stephanie felt tempted to dump some of the more unfair evaluations in the bin but wondered, resisting the urge, what she ought to do about the critical comments. She certainly did not have the time to spend ages rewriting the course with her research workload.

Recalling the last departmental committee meeting, she knew that 'quality' procedures had recently been overhauled and she was obliged to show in her 'action plan' how she would respond to these comments. Stephanie wondered whether she should cave in, make things easier for the students and 'spoon feed' them more with notes and handouts and 'lighten up' the assessment demands. She certainly knew that this was the strategy recommended by one of her more cynical colleagues who was concerned about students taking his specialist option in sufficient numbers. As he had said to Stephanie, somewhat sarcastically, 'It's a popularity contest these days, Steph. It's about entertainment value and meeting "customer" expectations. Just give them what they want. They won't thank you for working them too hard.' Stephanie had agreed that students seemed to expect everything to be put on a plate for them now rather than doing hard research as she had been expected to do in completing her degrees.

She was still wondering how she ought to respond to this set of critical evaluations as she made her way over to observe a lecture, by pre-arrangement with a colleague, as part of the department's 'quality enhancement' procedures. This required, among other things, reciprocal observations with a different colleague each academic year. Stephanie had certainly found it an eye-opener and had learnt a lot, she felt, in the process. The lecture turned out to be highly engaging and accomplished in many respects. It was well prepared and the students responded enthusiastically. They clearly found the lecturer, Max Schaefer, quite a charismatic speaker and, in fact, she knew that his course was extremely popular as he regularly got 'rave reviews' from students. However, Stephanie had qualms about its highly political nature. Max was overtly critical of a number of researchers and 'rubbished', she felt, the government's health-care research agenda. While he made a number of valid points, she was worried about over-generalizations which the students were apparently lapping up. When it came to questions from students towards the end, none of these sought to challenge the highly contentious nature of his lecture. She wondered, perhaps somewhat uncharitably, how well students would be treated if they wrote an essay or other assignment that took issue with his line of argument. While Stephanie needed to give Max some feedback following the observation, she knew, from previous contact with him, that he did not take kindly to criticism and that he was a firm believer in 'letting students know where I am coming from'. Looking at the teaching observation form she needed to fill in about 'pace of delivery', 'use of audiovisual equipment', etc there was certainly no need to raise the issue on paper.

Case study 4: Managing

Dr Dilip Patel has worked at The University of Broadlands as a Senior Lecturer in Mechanical Engineering for six years. He had started his lecturing job at the University after spending three years working as a volunteer for an international aid organization and a further period in the research and development department of a major corporation. Since starting at Broadlands the time seems to have flown by, although several of the papers he had planned to publish, based on his doctoral work on biofluidmechanics, were still languishing, half-written, on his hard drive. He had felt pretty swamped at first getting to grips with the demands of being a lecturer and taking responsibility for 'quality assurance' just prior to the inspection of the department last year. He had been surprised when, just before the beginning of term, he had been made the programme director of one of the department's major undergraduate degrees. The Head of Department had said that he was pleased by his progress and wanted to show his confidence in Dilip as a 'safe pair of hands' by giving him senior responsibility. When he had raised his concern about workload and his desire to become more research 'active', the Head had said it was important for him to 'pitch in' on administrative duties and gain experience as a programme director. Besides which, now that the inspection was over, he would be asking someone else in the department to take on the quality role.

Things seemed to be going satisfactorily so far in his new role. There had been a number of niggling problems with timetable clashes and complaints about rooming arrangements from students (too small, too hot, etc) but that, colleagues assured him, was quite normal. Today, though, had been a difficult one.

It all started in the most unexpected way with a knock at his office door. He had been pleased to see Claire Stevens, a bright and conscientious final-year student, who had rung to book the appointment with him a few days before. Relaxed, he leant back in his chair. He was not expecting the bombshell to come. Claire explained that she had come to see him about the marks received by the whole class for a particular module. This third-year module was one taught by Professor Bland, an experienced senior member of staff who had worked in the Department for over 20 years. The module was a final-year option for which Dilip had overall responsibility as programme director. Claire explained that she was there on behalf of the whole class even though she had not received a low mark herself. She had got 60 per cent. This took Dilip aback. He had become accustomed to individual students coming along on the odd occasion to complain about a low mark they had received for this or that assignment, but he had never encountered this situation. Claire went on to explain that hardly anyone in the group had received a mark above 40 per cent for that module's assignment and most students had got a mark of between 30 and 40 per cent. Many of the students, she said, who were accustomed to receiving average marks in the 50s and 60s, were concerned that this low mark would affect their degree result and could mean that several would fall below the class of degree they needed to secure conditional job and postgraduate study offers. When Dilip asked whether she or anyone else from the group had spoken with the module tutor, she replied that they had tried but had been rebuffed in a dismissive way. Dilip knew that the assignments had been second marked already and wondered what, if anything, he ought to do about the situation. Claire had not come to see him on her own behalf but for the benefit of others in the group, but there were clearly delicate issues here. Dilip recalled that he had recently over-heard part of an exchange between Professor Bland and a student while passing his office. He had heard Professor Bland saying, in a sarcastic and rhetorical way, 'I suggest you start by doing some reading. After all, if I am not mistaken, you're meant to be reading for a degree. Or don't students read these days?' Looking at his watch, Dilip realized that there were only five minutes to go before he was due to chair the Staff–Student Liaison Committee and, assuring Claire that he would get back to her, ended the meeting. Quite what he could do about this situation, though, was another matter.

Things went from bad to worse. The Staff–Student Committee did not go well. Despite explaining at the outset that the committee's role was to 'identify general issues and find practical solutions in a positive atmosphere', several of the student representatives had been quite scathing in their criticism of one of the teaching team, absent from the meeting. Although this member of staff was not mentioned by name, everyone present knew who was being talked about. The comments were clearly aimed at Dr Brunton, a part-time, visiting lecturer who had considerable expertise in his specialist field and was a busy, prac-tising professional. He was also a close personal friend of the Head of Department. They had known each other since studying at the same university back in the early 1970s and working together on post-doctoral work. The students complained that the second-year module for which Dr Brunton was responsible was badly organized and that lectures were frequently cancelled without notice. When they had tried to raise these issues with 'the module leader' (ie Dr Brunton), they had been told to 'grow up and start living in the real world!' Dilip responded that he would investigate the students' concerns, although privately he doubted that he would get very far. He was only too well aware of Dr Brunton's friendship with the Head of Department and, anyway, it would be hard to replace someone with Dr Brunton's expertise on a part-time basis. He hoped his response would help to take the heat out of what was rapidly becoming an increasingly tense atmosphere. Unfortunately, one of the student representatives pressed, 'so you will talk to Dr Brunton then?' At this point, the former programme director intervened sharply, telling the student that 'this is not the forum for making comments about individuals'. This remark led to an unexpected outburst from the third-year representative who said angrily: 'This meeting is just the usual farce. It's the same, year after year. We complained about Brunton last year and nothing happened. All you lecturers ever do is close ranks when anyone makes any criticism of your teaching. What's the point of this meeting? What's the point?' He then promptly walked out of the room. This incident caused a great deal of embarrassment and the meeting came to a fairly rapid conclusion. Resolving this issue and restoring the students' confidence in the work of the committee would clearly be no easy matter.

Back in his office, Dilip started to turn his mind to a different issue involving the teaching of a junior colleague on the degree programme for which he was responsible. This term, Dilip had been acting as a 'second marker' on Dr Greening's module and it had been something of a revelation. Dr Greening had been teaching at the university for the past 18 months and she had taken over a well-established module from a senior member of the department who had recently retired. Dr Greening had made substantial changes to the module, increasing the use of active learning techniques, group work and the use of technical reports in assessment to reflect the challenges of professional practice. These innovations had been popular with students. This year substantially more students had chosen to undertake her module. As a result, some of the more traditionally organized modules, using lectures and laboratory work and assessed largely by individual assignments and examinations, had recruited poorly. Also, the rate of innovation on Dr

Greening's module was such that it no longer conformed to departmental rules and procedures. The examination had been scrapped
and the assessment was now completely by coursework. This
consisted of a group technical report, a group oral presentation and a
mark awarded to students on the basis of their 'contribution in class'.
While Dilip wanted to encourage innovation, he did not want it to
backfire and alienate colleagues in quite a traditional and conservative
teaching environment. The loss of students to Dr Greening's module
had already caused some resentment among other staff and moves
were afoot within the department to bring the assessment of the
module back into line with departmental procedures by raising the
issue at the next departmental Board of Studies. Questions had been
raised about how the external examiner could verify student achievement on the basis of oral presentations and 'class contribution' grades,
among other criticisms. Dr Greening clearly had a lot to contribute to
the development of the department's teaching but Dilip needed to
speak with her and find a way forward to sort out this issue before
matters came to a head.

References

Ainley, P (1994) *Degrees of Difference: Higher education in the 1990s*, Lawrence and Wishart, London

Alderman, G (2000) Teaching and research in higher education, *Reflections on Higher Education*, **11**, pp 26–34

Allen, M (1988) *The Goals of Universities*, The Society for Research into Higher Education/Open University Press, Milton Keynes

Ashby, E (1969) A Hippocratic oath for the academic profession, *Minerva*, **8** (1), Reports and Documents, pp 64–66

Ashworth, P, Bannister, P and Thorne, P (1997) Guilty in whose eyes? University students' perceptions of cheating and plagiarism in academic work and assessment, *Studies in Higher Education*, **22** (2), pp 187–203

Badley, G (2002) A really useful link between teaching and research, *Teaching in Higher Education*, **7** (4), pp 443–455

Banks, A and Banks, S P (eds) (1998) *Fiction and Social Science: By ice or fire*, AltaMira Press, London

Barnes, L, Christensen, C R and Hansen, A B (1994) *Teaching and the Case Method*, Harvard Business School, Boston

Barnett, R (1990) *The Idea of a Higher Education*, The Society for Research into Higher Education/Open University Press, Buckingham

Barnett, R (1992) *Improving Higher Education: Total Quality Care*, The Society for Research into Higher Education/Open University Press, Buckingham

Becher, T and Kogan, M (1992) *Process and Structure in Higher Education*, Routledge, London

Becher, T and Trowler, P (2001) *Academic Tribes and Territories: Intellectual enquiry and the cultures of disciplines*, Society for Research into Higher Education/Open University Press, Buckingham

Bennett, B (2002) Exiting gladly, Letter to the *Times Higher Education Supplement*, 29 November, p 17

Berlak, A and Berlak, H (1981) *Dilemmas of Schooling*, Methuen, London

Berry, A (1995) Smoother learning par for the course, *The Times Higher Education Supplement*, 10 November, p 13

Blackstone, T (1998) View from the national perspective, in *Development Training for Academics: Proceedings of a conference held by Goldsmiths College University of London*, 26 March, ed K Gregory, pp 1–3, Goldsmiths College, London

Blaxter, L, Hughes, C and Tight, M (1998) *The Academic Career Handbook*, Open University Press, Buckingham

Bligh, D (1998) *What's the Use of Lectures?*, Intellect Books, Exeter

Bligh, D, Thomas, H and McNay, I (1999) *Understanding Higher Education*, Intellect Books, Exeter

Blum, L A (1980) *Friendship, Altruism and Morality*, Routledge and Kegan Paul, London

Bono, de E (1976) *Teaching Thinking*, Penguin, Harmondsworth

Booth, A (1997) Listening to students: experiences and expectations in the transition to a history degree, *Studies in Higher Education*, **22** (2), pp 205–20

Booth, C, Bowie, S, Jordan, J and Rippin, A (2000) The use of the case study method in large and diverse undergraduate business programmes: problems and issues, *The International Journal of Management Education*, **1** (1), pp 62–75

Bourner, T and Flowers, S (1997) Teaching and learning methods in higher education: a glimpse of the future, *Reflections on Higher Education*, **9**, pp 77–102

Bourner, J, Hughes, M and Bourner, T (2001) First-year undergraduate experiences of group project work, *Assessment and Evaluation in Higher Education*, **26** (1), pp 19–39

Boyer, E L (1990) *Scholarship Reconsidered: Priorities of the professoriate*, Carnegie Foundation for the Advancement of Teaching, Princeton

Bridgstock, M (1996) Ethics at the interface: academic scientists' views of ethical and unethical behaviour involving industrial links, *Industry and Higher Education*, **10** (5), pp 275–84

Brindley, C and Scoffield, S (1998) Peer assessment in undergraduate programmes, *Teaching in Higher Education*, **3** (1), pp 79–89

Brockbank, A and McGill, I (1998) *Facilitating Reflective Learning in Higher Education*, The Society for Research into Higher Education/Open University Press, Buckingham

Brockett, M (1997) Moral development or moral decline? A discussion of ethics education for the health care professions, *Medical Teacher*, **19** (4), pp 301–09

Brookfield, S D (1987) *Developing Critical Thinkers*, Open University Press, Milton Keynes

Brown, S and Glasner, A (1999) *Assessment Matters in Higher Education*, The Society for Research into Higher Education/Open University Press, Buckingham

Cahn, S M (1986) *Saints and Scamps: Ethics in academia*, Rowman and Littlefield, Totowa, NJ

Carbone, P F (ed) (1987) *Value Theory and Education*, Krieger Publishing Co, Malabar, FL

Carnegie Commission on Higher Education (1973) *The Purposes and the Performance of Higher Education in the United States*, McGraw-Hill, London

Carter, I (1990) *Ancient Cultures of Conceit: British university fiction in the post-war years*, Routledge, London

Centra, J A (1993) *Reflective Faculty Evaluation: Enhancing teaching and determining faculty effectiveness*, Jossey-Bass, San Francisco

Cheng, J Y S (1995) Higher education in Hong Kong – the approach of 1997 and the China factor, *Higher Education*, **30** (3), pp 257–71

Chryssides, G and Kaler, J (1996) *Essentials of Business Ethics*, McGraw-Hill, London

Clouder, L (1998) Getting the 'right answers': student evaluation as a reflection of intellectual development, *Teaching in Higher Education*, **3** (2), pp 185–95

Coate, K, Barnett, R and Williams, G (2001) Relationships between teaching and research in higher education in England, *Higher Education Quarterly*, **55** (2), pp 158–74

Coates, N and Koerner, R (1996) How market oriented are business studies degrees?, *Journal of Marketing Management*, **12**, pp 455–75

Cummins, J (1999) *The Teaching of Business Ethics At Undergraduate, Postgraduate and Professional Levels in the UK: A survey and report*, Institute of Business Ethics, London

Curzon-Hobson, A (2002) A pedagogy of trust in higher education, *Teaching in Higher Education*, **7** (3), pp 265–76

D'Andrea, V and Gosling, D (2001) Joining the dots: reconceptualizing educational development, *Active Learning in Higher Education*, **2** (2), pp 64–80

Dearlove, J (1995) Collegiality, managerialism and leadership in English universities, *Tertiary Education and Management*, **1** (2), pp 161–69

Department for Education and Skills (2003) *The Future of Higher Education: Creating opportunity, releasing potential, achieving excellence*, The Stationery Office, London

Doherty, B (1996) Points from an ethical debate arising from the provision of learning support for disabled students in higher education, *British Journal of Special Education*, **23** (1), pp 162–65

Easterby-Smith, M, Thorpe, R and Lowe, A (1991) *Management Research: An introduction*, Sage, London

Elton, L (2001) Training for a craft or a profession?, *Teaching in Higher Education*, **6** (3), pp 421–22

Eraut, M (1994) *Developing Professional Knowledge and Competence*, Falmer Press, London

Evans, K R, Ferris, S P and Thompson, G R (1998) Ethics and the ivory tower: the case of academic departments of finance, *Teaching Business Ethics*, **2** (1), pp 17–34

Fisch, L (ed) (1996) *Ethical Dimensions of College and University Teaching: Understanding and honouring the special relationship between teachers and students*, Jossey-Bass, San Francisco

Fleming, A (1995) Accounting education: the place of ethics in the curriculum and the consequences of its omission, *Journal of Further and Higher Education in Scotland*, **19** (1), pp 18–21

Foot, P (1978) *Virtues and Vices and Other Essays in Moral Philosophy*, Blackwell, Oxford

Forsyth, D R (1980) A taxonomy of ethical ideologies, *Journal of Personality and Social Psychology*, **39** (1), pp 175–84

Fox, M F (1992) Research, teaching and publication productivity: mutuality versus competition in academia, *Sociology of Education*, **65**(4), pp 293–305

Franklyn-Stokes, A and Newstead, S E (1995) Undergraduate cheating: who does what and why?, *Studies in Higher Education*, **20** (2), pp 159–72

Freire, P (1997) *Teachers as Cultural Workers: Letters to those that dare teach*, tr D Macedo, D Koike and A Oliveira, Westview Press, Boulder

French, N J, Massey, W F and Young, K (2001) Research assessment in Hong Kong, *Higher Education*, **42** (1), pp 35–46

Fry, H, Ketteridge, S and Marshall, S (eds) (1999) *A Handbook of Teaching and Learning in Higher Education*, Kogan Page, London

Gardner, R, Cairns, J and Lawton, D (eds) (2000) *Education for Values*, Kogan Page, London

Gibbs, G (2002) Institutional strategies for linking research and teaching, *Exchange*, **3**, pp 8–11

Goleman, D (1995) *Emotional Intelligence: Why it can matter more than IQ*, Bloomsbury, London

Goodlad, S (1997) *The Quest for Quality: Sixteen forms of heresy in higher education*, The Society for Research into Higher Education/Open University Press, Buckingham

Gordon, G (1997) Preparing and developing academics for the needs of effective provision in mass tertiary education, *Higher Education Management*, **9** (3), pp 67–78

Grant, R (1997) A claim for the case method in the teaching of geography, *Journal of Geography in Higher Education*, **21** (2), pp 171–85

Grauerholz, E and Copenhaver, S (1994) When the personal becomes problematic: the ethics of using experiential teaching methods, *Teaching Sociology*, **22**, pp 319–27

Grinnell, F (2002) The impact of ethics on research, *The Chronicle of Higher Education*, 4 October, p B15

Gross Davis, B (1993) *Tools for Teaching*, Jossey-Bass, San Francisco

Habeshaw, S, Habeshaw, T and Gibbs, G (1992) *53 Interesting Things to Do in Your Seminars and Tutorials*, 4th edn, Technical and Educational Services Ltd, Bristol

Halsey, A H (1992) *Decline of Donnish Dominion*, Clarendon, Oxford

Hanson, K (1996) Between apathy and advocacy: teaching and modelling ethical reflection, in *Ethical Dimensions of College and University Teaching: Understanding and honouring the special relationship between teachers and students*, ed L Fisch, pp 33–45, Jossey-Bass, San Francisco

Hargreaves, A (1994) *Changing Teachers, Changing Times*, Cassell, London

Harley, S (2002) The impact of research selectivity on academic work and identity in UK universities, *Studies in Higher Education*, **27** (2), pp 187–205

Harman, G (2000) Allocating research infrastructure grants in post-binary higher education systems: British and Australian approaches, *Journal of Higher Education Policy and Management*, **22** (2), pp 111–26

Holloway, R (1999) *Godless Morality: Keeping religion out of ethics*, Canongate, Edinburgh

Hooks, B (1994) *Teaching to Transgress: Education as the practice of freedom*, Routledge, New York

Horgan, J (1999) Lecturing for learning, in *A Handbook for Teaching and Learning in Higher Education*, eds H Fry, S Ketteridge and S Marshall, pp 83–94, Kogan Page, London

Jarvis, P (1983) *Professional Education*, Croom Helm, London

Jenkins, A, Blackman, T, Lindsay, R and Paton-Saltzberg, R (1998) Teaching and research: student perspectives and policy implications, *Studies in Higher Education*, **23** (2), pp 127–41

Jensen, K (2001) International business, in *Effective Learning and Teaching in Business and Management*, ed B Macfarlane and R Ottewill, pp 123–137, Kogan Page, London

Johnson, R (2000) The authority of the Student Evaluation Questionnaire, *Teaching in Higher Education*, **5** (4), pp 419–34

Kant, I (1964) *Groundwork of the Metaphysic of Morals*, tr H J Paton, Harper and Row, London

Kant, I (1979) *The Conflict of the Faculties*, tr M J McGregor, University of Nebraska Press, Lincoln

Keeson, F, Wubbels, T, van Tartwijk, J and Bouhuijs, P (1996) Preparing university teachers in The Netherlands: issues and trends, *International Journal of Academic Development*, 1 (2), pp 8–16

Keig, L (2000) Formative peer review of teaching: attitudes of faculty at liberal arts colleges toward colleague assessment, *Journal of Personnel Evaluation in Education*, **14** (1), pp 67–87

Keith-Spiegel, P, Wittig, A F, Perkins, D V, Balogh, D W and Whitley, B E (1996) Intervening with colleagues, in *Ethical Dimensions of College and University Teaching: Understanding and honouring the special relationship between teachers and students*, ed L Fisch, pp 75–78, Jossey-Bass, San Francisco

Kennedy, B D (1997) *Academic Duty*, Harvard University Press, Harvard

Kjonstad, B and Willmott, H (1995) Business ethics: restrictive or empowering?, *Journal of Business Ethics*, **14**, pp 445–64

Kneale, P (1997) The rise of the 'strategic student': how can we adapt to cope?, in *Facing Up to Radical Changes in Universities and Colleges*, ed S Armstrong, G Thompson and S Brown, pp 119–30, Kogan Page/SEDA, London

Knight, P T (2002) *Being a Teacher in Higher Education*, The Society for Research into Higher Education/Open University Press, Buckingham

Knight, P T and Trowler, P R (2000) Department-level cultures and the improvement of learning and teaching, *Studies in Higher Education*, **25** (1), pp 69–83

Kolitch, E and Dean, A V (1999) Student ratings of instruction in the USA: hidden assumptions and missing conceptions about 'good' teaching, *Studies in Higher Education*, **24** (1), pp 27–42

Kreber, C (2001) Learning experientially through case studies? A conceptual analysis, *Teaching in Higher Education*, **6** (2), pp 217–28

Kreisberg, S (1992) *Transforming Power: Domination, empowerment, and education*, State University of New York, New York

Krushke, J K (1998) *Teaching as an expression of liberty*, Talk presented at the 31st Annual Meeting of the Society for Mathematical Psychology, Vanderbilt University, Nashville, Tennessee, 8 August

Laffin, M (1986) *Professionalism and Policy: The role of the professions in the central–local government relationship*, Gower, Aldershot

Laurillard, D (1993) *Rethinking University Teaching: A framework for effective use of educational technology*, Routledge, London

Layer, G (2002) Developing inclusivity, *International Journal of Lifelong Education*, **21** (1), pp 3–12

Ledic, J, Rafajac, B and Kovac, V (1999) Assessing the quality of university teaching in Croatia, *Teaching in Higher Education*, **4** (2), pp 213–33

Lovelock, C, Vandermerwe, S and Lewis, B (1996) *Services Marketing: A European perspective*, Prentice Hall, London

Lyon, P M and Hendry, G D (2002) The use of the Course Experience Questionnaire as a monitoring evaluation tool in a problem-based medical programme, *Assessment and Evaluation in Higher Education*, **27** (4), pp 339–52

Macfarlane, B (2001) Justice and lecturer professionalism, *Teaching in Higher Education*, **6** (2), pp 141–52

Macfarlane, B (2002) Dealing with Dave's dilemma's: exploring the ethics of pedagogic practice, *Teaching in Higher Education*, **7** (2), pp 167–78

MacIntyre, A (1981) *After Virtue*, Duckworth, London

MacIntyre, A (1990) *Three Rival Versions of Moral Enquiry*, Duckworth, London

Malcolm, J and Zukas, M (2001) Bridging pedagogic gaps: conceptual discontinuities in higher education, *Teaching in Higher Education*, **6** (1), pp 33–42

Marsh, A (2001) Blind date leads to a canny union, *Times Higher Education Supplement*, 31 August, p 14

McKee, C and Belson, S (1990) The ombudsman in Canadian universities: and justice for all, *Studies in Higher Education*, **15** (2), pp 197–206

Mintz, S M (1996) Aristotelian virtue and business ethics, *Journal of Business Ethics*, **15**, pp 827–38

Moodie, G (1996) On justifying the different claims to academic freedom, *Minerva*, **34**, pp 124–50

Morgan, E and Rooney, M (1997) Can dyslexic students be trained as teachers?, *Support for Learning*, **12** (1), pp 28–31

Morris, T (1995) Professionalism, in *The Blackwell Encyclopaedic Dictionary of Organizational Behavior*, ed N Nicholson, pp 449–50, Blackwell, Oxford

Mortiboys, A (2002) *The Emotionally Intelligent Lecturer*, Staff and Educational Development Association, Birmingham

Murray, H, Gillese, E, Lennon, M, Mercer, P and Robinson, M (1996) Ethical principles for College and University teaching, in *Ethical Dimensions of College and University Teaching: Understanding and honouring the special relationship between teachers and students*, ed L Fisch, pp 57–63, Jossey-Bass, San Francisco

National Committee of Inquiry into Higher Education (1997) *Higher Education in the Learning Society: Report of the National Committee*, HMSO, London

Nelson, C and Watt, S (1999) *Academic Keywords: A Devil's Dictionary for Higher Education*, Routledge, London

Niblett, W R (1955) *Education – The Lost Dimension*, William Sloane Associates, New York

Nixon, J (1996) Professional identity and the restructuring of higher education, *Studies in Higher Education*, **21** (1), pp 5–16

Nixon, J (2001) Towards a new academic professionalism: a manifesto of hope, *British Journal of Sociology of Education*, **22** (2), pp 227–44

Nolan, M P (1997) *Standards in Public Life: First report on Standards in Public Life*, HMSO, London

November, P (1997) Learning to teach experientially: a pilgrim's progress, *Studies in Higher Education*, **22** (2), pp 289–99

Oakley, J (1992) *Morality and the Emotions*, Routledge, London

Orsini, J L (1988) Halo effects in student evaluation of faculty: a case application, *Journal of Marketing Education*, **10** (2), pp 220–23

Ottewill, R (2001) Tutors as professional role models with particular reference to undergraduate business education, *Higher Education Quarterly*, **55** (4), pp 436–51

Parry, G and Houghton, D (1996) Plagiarism in UK universities, *Education and the Law*, **8** (3), pp 201–215

Partington, J (1994) Double-marking students' work, *Assessment and Evaluation in Higher Education*, **19** (1), pp 57–60

Piercy, N F, Lane, N and Peters, L D (1997) The validity and reliability of student evaluations of courses and faculty in British business schools, *Journal of European Business Education*, **6** (2), pp 72–84

Pincoffs, E (1986) *Quandaries and Virtues: Against reductivism in ethics*, University Press of Kansas, Kansas

Piper, D W (1992) Are professors professional?, *Higher Education Quarterly*, **46** (2), pp 143–56

Poe, R E (2000) Hitting a nerve: when touchy subjects come up in class, *Observer* 13 (9), pp 18–19, 31

Postle, G and Sturman, A (2000) Models of learning as a factor in on-line education: an Australian case study, Unpublished conference paper, *Innovation and Creativity in Teaching and Learning*, 12–13 June, University of Stirling

Pring, R (2001) The virtues and vices of an educational researcher, *Journal of Philosophy of Education*, **35** (3), pp 407–21

Pumphrey, P (1998) Reforming policy and provision for dyslexic students in higher education: towards a national code of practice, *Support for Learning*, **13** (2), pp 87–90

Race, P (1998) *500 Tips for Open and Flexible Learning*, Kogan Page, London

Raffe, D (1994) Modular strategies for overcoming academic/vocational divisions: issues arising from the Scottish experience, *Journal of Education Policy*, **9** (2), pp 141–54

Ramsden, P (1992) *Learning to Teach in Higher Education*, Routledge, London

Reid, I and Parker, F (1995) Whatever happened to the sociology of education in teacher education?, *Educational Studies*, **21** (3), pp 395–413

Rippin, A, Booth, C, Bowie, S and Jordan, J (2002) A complex case: using the case method to explore uncertainty and ambiguity in undergraduate business education, *Teaching in Higher Education*, **7** (4), pp 429–41

Ritzer, G (1998) *The McDonalization Thesis*, Sage, London

Robbins, Lord (1963) *Higher Education: Report of the committee appointed by the Prime Minister under the chairmanship of Lord Robbins 1961–1963*, HMSO, London

Rodabaugh, R (1996) Institutional commitment to fairness in college teaching, in *Ethical Dimensions of College and University Teaching: Understanding and honouring the special relationship between teachers and students*, ed Fisch, L, pp 37–45, Jossey-Bass, San Francisco

Rodabaugh, R and Kravitz, D (1994) Effects of procedural fairness on student judgments of professors, *Journal of Excellence in College Teaching*, **5** (2), pp 67–83

Roselle, A (1996) The case study method: a learning tool for practising librarians and information specialists, *Library Review*, **45** (4), pp 30–38

Rowland, S (1999) The role of theory in a pedagogical model for lecturers in higher education, *Studies in Higher Education*, **24** (3), pp 303–14

Rowland, S (2000) *The Enquiring University Teacher*, SHRE/Open University Press, Buckingham

Rowland, S (2002) Overcoming fragmentation in professional life: the challenge for academic development, *Higher Education Quarterly*, **56** (1), pp 52–64

Rowland, S, Byron, C, Furedi, F, Padfield, N and Smyth, T (1998) Turning academics into teachers?, *Teaching in Higher Education*, **3** (2), pp 133–41

Russell, C (1993) *Academic Freedom*, Routledge, London

Ryle, G (1972) Can virtue be taught?, in *Education and Development of Reason*, ed R F Dearden, P H Hirst and R S Peters, pp 434–47, Routledge and Kegan Paul, London

Sachs, J (2000) The activist professional, *Journal of Educational Change*, **1** (1), pp 77–95

Saunders, G and Weible, R (1999) Electronic courses: old wine in new bottles?, *Internet Research: Electronic networking applications and policy*, **9** (5), pp 339–47

Schon, D (1983) *The Reflective Practitioner: How professionals think in action*, Basic Books, New York

Schon, D (1987) *Educating the Reflective Practitioner*, Jossey-Bass, San Francisco

Scott, I (2002) *Policy dilemmas in shaping higher education for the realities of globalisation: the case of South Africa*, City University, Annual Higher Education Policy Lecture, London, unpublished

Scott, P (1995) *The Meanings of Mass Higher Education*, Society for Research into Higher Education/Open University Press, Buckingham

Scott, P (ed) (1998) *The Globalization of Higher Education*, Society for Research into Higher Education/Open University Press, Buckingham

Scott, S V (1999) The academic as service provider: is the customer 'always right'?, *Journal of Higher Education Policy and Management*, **21** (2), pp 193–202

Seldin, P (1993) The use and abuse of student ratings of professors, *The Chronicle of Higher Education*, 21 July, p A40

Shils, E (1982) The academic ethic, *Minerva*, **20** (1–2), pp 107–208

Simon, H A (1957) *Models of Man*, Wiley, London

Small, R (2001) Codes are not enough: what philosophy can contribute to the ethics of educational research, *Journal of Philosophy of Education*, **35** (3), pp 387–406

Solomon, R C (1992) *Ethics and Excellence*, Oxford University Press, Oxford

Staniforth, D and Harland, T (1999) The work of an academic: Jack of all trades, or master of one?, *International Journal for Academic Development*, **4** (2), pp 142–49

Stone, C and Wehlage, G (1982) Four persisting school dilemmas, *Action in Teacher Education*, **4**, pp 17–30

Strike, K A (1990) Teaching ethics to teachers: what the curriculum should be about, *Teaching and Teacher Education*, **6** (1), pp 47–53

Strike, K A and Soltis, J F (1992) *The Ethics of Teaching*, 2nd edn, Teachers College Press, New York

Talib, A (2001) The continuing behavioural modification of academics since the 1992 Research Assessment Exercise, *Higher Education Review*, **33** (3), pp 30–46

Talib, A and Steele, A (2000) The Research Assessment Exercise: strategies and trade-offs, *Higher Education Quarterly*, **54** (1), pp 68–87

Thomas, H G (2001) Funding mechanism or quality assessment: responses to the Research Assessment Exercise in English institutions, *Journal of Higher Education Policy and Management*, **23** (2), pp 171–79

Timpson, W W and Andrew, D (1997) Rethinking student evaluations and the improvement of teaching: instruments for change at the University of Queensland, *Studies in Higher Education*, **22** (1), pp 55–65

Tomlinson, J and Little, V (2000) A code of the ethical principles underlying teaching as a professional activity, in *Education for Values*, ed R Gardner, J Cairns and D Lawton, pp 147–57, Kogan Page, London

Trowler, P (1997) Beyond the Robbins trap: reconceptualising academic responses to change in higher education (or... Quiet Flows the Don?), *Studies in Higher Education*, **22** (3), pp 301–18

United Kingdom Central Council for Nursing, Midwifery and Health Visiting (1986) *Project 2000: A new preparation for practice*, UKCC, London

Van der Vorst, R (1998) Engineering, ethics and professionalism, *European Journal of Engineering Education*, **23** (2), pp 171–79

Velayutham, S and Perera, H (1993) The reflective accountant: towards a new model for professional development, *Accounting Education*, **2** (4), pp 287–301

Walker, J (1998) Student plagiarism in universities: what are we doing about it?, *Higher Education Research and Development*, **17** (1), pp 89–106

Walker, M (2001) *Reconstructing Professionalism in University Teaching*, The Society for Research into Higher Education/Open University Press, Buckingham

Watson, D and Bowden, R (2000) *After Dearing: A mid term report*, University of Brighton, Brighton

Watson, D and Taylor, R (1998) *Lifelong Learning and the University: A Post-Dearing Agenda*, Falmer Press, London

Watson, T J (2000) Ethnographic fiction science: making sense of managerial work and organisational research, *Organization*, **7** (3), pp 489–510

Weber, C (1995) *Stories of Virtue in Business*, University of Press of America, Lanham

Whicker, M L and Kronenfeld, J J (1994) *Dealing with Ethical Dilemmas on Campus*, Sage, London

Whitley, B E and Keith-Spiegel, P (2002) *Academic Dishonesty: An Educator's Guide*, Lawrence Erlbaum Associates, Mahwah, NJ

Wilson, K L, Lizzio, A and Ramsden, P (1997) The development, validation and application of the Course Experience Questionnaire, *Studies in Higher Education*, **22** (1), pp 33–53

Winter, R (1996) New liberty, new discipline: academic work in the new higher education, in *Working in Higher Education*, ed R Cuthbert, pp 71–83, The Society for Research into Higher Education/Open University Press, Buckingham

Index